ANOTHER UNIVERSITY
IS POSSIBLE

—ANOTHER UNIVERSITY IS POSSIBLE EDITORIAL COLLECTIVE—
Luis Alvarez, Roberto Alvarez, Cutler Edwards, Stevie Ruiz,
Elizabeth Sine, Maki Smith, and Daniel Widener

University Readers™
San Diego, CA

Copyright © 2010 University Readers Inc. All rights reserved. No part of this publication may be reprinted, reproduced, transmitted, or utilized in any form or by any electronic, mechanical, or other means, now known or hereafter invented, including photocopying, microfilming, and recording, or in any information retrieval system without the written permission of University Readers, Inc.

First published in the United States of America in 2010 by University Readers, Inc.

Trademark Notice: Product or corporate names may be trademarks or registered trademarks, and are used only for identification and explanation without intent to infringe.

15 14 13 12 11   1 2 3 4 5

Printed in the United States of America

ISBN: 978-1609279-47-9

University Readers™
800.200.3908 I www.universityreaders.com

CONTENTS

PART 3 CONSTELLATIONS OF STRUGGLE

PART 4 FUTURES

FOREWORD

Another University Is Possible Editorial Collective

B etween February 15 and March 4, 2010, students, staff, and faculty at the University of California, San Diego (UCSD) mobilized against a well-publicized sequence of racist acts on campus and the on-going privatization of higher education. Building occupations and mass rallies, media campaigns and strategic debates were all part of the ebb and flow of a movement that faced three opponents: an inept administration; a student body riddled with ignorance and racism; and decades of active hostility directed by California voters against communities of color and the idea of equality in the Golden State.

The social force that came together in the spring of 2010 drew upon the historical legacies of earlier efforts to create a Lumumba-Zapata College; to force the University of California to divest from apartheid-era South Africa; and to create a Cross Cultural Center that would serve as a space of organizing and refuge during the bleak landscape of the Bush-Clinton years. At the same time, what took place during the spring of 2010 was powerfully *new*: a model of coalitional, improvisational, multiethnic organizing that rejected the university's deployment of "diversity" as a rhetorical device and exposed the economic-structural conditions and misguided administrative priorities that failed to ensure an equitable and accessible campus. At the core of this movement lay three interlocking dynamics: the foresight and tenacity of a Black Student Union (BSU) convinced of the necessity and possibility of change; a passionate unity of vision and purpose—a revolutionary trust—between the BSU and the Movimiento Estudiantil Chicano de Aztlán (MEChA); and the ability of BSU/MECHA to serve as the spark for a wider explosion capable of incorporating the hopes and rage of Asian/Pacific Islander and Native American students, progressive whites, and those segments of the UCSD campus engaged in a wider fight against the ongoing privatization of higher education in California.

At the same time, the events at UCSD in the winter of 2010 illustrate the tenacity of what Vijay Prashad has termed "multiracism." Consider the following about the racist provocations that shook the campus: defenders of the so-called "Compton Cookout" argued that African Americans were in attendance at the original fraternity party; the editorial board of the racist *Koala* newspaper contained a majority of students of color; the noose hung in Geisel library was placed there by a Latina. Moreover, the demographics of the campus—UCSD's student body is 49% Asian/Asian American, 13% Latina/o, 1.3% African American, and 0.4% Native American and UCSD's faculty are 78% white, 15% Asian/Asian American, and 7% combined Latina/o, African American, and Native American—prompted many of the same sorts of questions about race that were raised in the aftermath of the 1992 Rodney King riots. The materials collected within this book represent a genealogy of what one version of a post-colorblind social movement for racial justice looks like.

The students also confronted the enormous burden of the dead hand of history. In its fifty-year existence, the black student percentage of UC San Diego has never exceeded 3%. In an institution fixated on the sciences, humanistic inquiry of social inequality rarely found an echo across the campus. In a place helping to pioneer the model of using public resources in the service of private capital, this movement emerged to demand a University committed to the values of access and equality—a University that puts people before profits.

As a snapshot of a movement and a moment, this collection deliberately avoids the presentation of a straightforward, linear narrative. Instead, the speeches, poems, statements, blog commentary and photographs within are meant to capture the contours and dynamism of this struggle during these few short weeks. In presenting a collection of various voices, we hope to play a role in disrupting the "official" narrative of events, rejecting the idea that the problems began with the Compton Cookout and concluded with the administrative agreement to begin to implement the demands put forth by the Black Student Union. Here, we take our lead from the students, who rightly maintain that what we have witnessed began before we were here, and will continue after we—as editors, students, faculty, and staff—have moved on.

Growing from this shared belief that "Another University is Possible," we hope this book plays a small part in much broader efforts to document the growing movement for racial and social justice at UCSD; compliment, help sustain, and regenerate the racial justice movement at UCSD; and serve as a research, teaching, and organizing resource for use by students, staff, and faculty at UCSD and beyond engaged in the study of race, the university, and collaborative social change. We see the recent events at UCSD—from the original racist acts to the political mobilizations against them to the blowback against the mobilizations—as an opportune moment to begin thinking about how newly articulated racisms in a time of declared "colorblindness" combine exclusion, insult, and violence against communities of color, at the same time giving rise to new forms of alliance, solidarity, and transformative movements. In this light, we also understand the events of late February and early March 2010 as the beginning, not end, of a protracted struggle to make UCSD a better university. It is in this spirit of continued struggle that we offer this book as a piece of the on-going racial justice movement, a conversation starter for future movements, and one reminder that UCSD can be a more equitable and racially just place of higher learning.

PART 1

BEYOND THE COOKOUT

Photo courtesy of Erik Jepsen.

UCSD Black Student Union Address! State of Emergency!

Black Student Union Statement, February 2010

It is with crucial concern and urgency that I write this letter to bring to your attention the state of the campus climate for African-American students at UC San Diego. The University is allowing the African-American students to be racially demoralized by a group of students on this campus. The most recent incident was February 18, 2010 between 11:00pm and midnight a group of students on the UC San Diego Student Run Television Program (SR-TV) making statements in support of the racial "Compton cookout" party That took place this past Monday February 15, 2010. These students insulted the African-American community by stating "you ungrateful niggers ...". It is a toxic environment for African-American students on this campus. The SR-TV is funded by the University so in fact, it is using taxpayers dollars to degrade and demoralize the African-American students and other underrepresented backgrounds as well. Again, this is a STATE OF EMERGENCY the University is in direct violation of its "Principles of Community". Students do not feel safe on this campus and it is affecting their everyday lives. We need direct action from the University immediately.

Those students involved in the shameful racist acts should be suspended from the University for spreading such hateful messages about the African-American community to the University campus-wide and with the University's funding and approval. These types of acts will not be tolerated. The Black Student Union calls you to support us in this struggle to heal the underrepresented student community and to create a healthier campus climate at UC San Diego. Students are exhausted and tired of bailing this institution out by developing our own student initiated outreach, retention, and yield efforts and maintaining and sustaining them with our own student fees. When will the University do its part? Time for change is long overdue it's the University's turn to create that change.

Please understand that this tragedy has marked UC San Diego as a racist University and consequently damaged our student initiated yield efforts we worked on this entire academic year. We demand as a result of this dilemma the University take full responsibility for these actions occurring and take direct action to heal a community that has been scarred. Several students and their families are considering transferring out of UC San Diego because of this injustice. We can no longer stand this HOSTILE ENVIRONMENT. Please Come Support our Protest and march to the Chancellors office today February 19th at 9am on Library Walk at UCSD.

The demands of the Black Student Union to address the issue of poor campus climate are stated below and are to be effective immediately.

- We demand a Permanent Task Force to fund more outreach efforts and create more opportunities for hiring African-American Faculty.
- We demand the University fully fund the traditional and non-traditional events of the Black Student Union in our efforts to create a better climate for ourselves.
- Match Funds with Student Promoted Access Center for Education and Service (SPACES) budget including the Student Initiated Access Program and Services (SIAPS) and Academic Success Program (ASP) budgets. Black Student Union Statement February 2010 .
- We demand that every time the freshmen class enrollment is cut the University matches the student fees that they would have been paying to SPACES permanently to SPACES.
- We demand that Chancellor Fox uses more energy and resources to providing research based scholarships for

African-American students as apart of a retention component from the Chancellor's Diversity Office.

- Demand the University to increase the African-American populations in all areas of the campus including, Students (undergraduates and graduates), PhD Candidates, Faculty, Staff and Administration.
- We demand the University directly fully fund Faculty-Student Mentor Programs.
- We demand the University staff the vacant Program Coordinator position of the African-American Studies Minor .
- We demand the Chancellor's office make the African-American Studies Minor and the Chicano Latina/o Arts and Humanities Minor a priority for the University.
- We demand the University to charge a Task Force to create the plan for an African-American Resource Center on Campus in two years to provide a safe space for the African-American community.
- We demand that Chancellor Fox create an Office for Diversity Affairs from her administration instead of a part-time position with a title.
- We demand the Chancellor fully funds the Chief Diversity Office.
- We demand a change of Admissions Policy from a Comprehensive to a Holistic Review beginning for the Fall 2011 applicant pool.
- We demand campus climate becomes the Chancellor's number one priority, especially in this time of crisis.
- We demand Chancellor Fox and the University have mutual respect of the "Principles of Community" and create a precedent of prioritizing students of color and leading by example. When demand that there be repercussions when the "Principles of Community" are blatantly being violated.
- We demand the Chancellor's Office charges the Campus Climate Commission that will work primarily on improving the campus climate and providing a safer and more

welcoming space and experience for the students of under-represented communities and the entire student body.

- We demand a permanent quarterly and annual campus climate report from this Campus Climate Commission. This Campus Climate Commission must report directly to SAAC.
- We demand the University create a space in the central part of campus safe for African-American students on campus.
- We demand the Chancellor, Vice Chancellor of Student Affairs, and Vice Chancellor of Academic Affairs, Chief Diversity Office meet with the chair and vice chair of the Black Student Union at least once every academic quarter.
- We demand the University provide financial education and counseling, teaching students from low-income, under-privileged communities how to manage their money being independent college students.
- We demand that the University sends out a campus-wide email presenting the Black Student Union's Do UC us? Campaign Report on Yield of African-American students immediately.
- We demand the University live up to it's "Principles of Community" and show leadership and integrity by giving up the remains of the Kumeeay tribe and respect the native land on which we are housed.
- We demand three permanent designated spaces for African-American inspired art to reflect the struggle and progress for students of color on this campus.
- We demand that Chancellor Fox fully funds this Art space. We demand that the moral "Chicano Legacy" become a permanent art piece on this campus. We demand that Native American, Latino and Asian-Pacific Islander cultural art is reflected publicly on this campus.
- We demand Chancellor Fox and the Vice Chancellor of Academic Affairs, and the Academic Senate mandate a diversity sensitivity requirement for every undergraduate student to take an African-American studies, Ethnic Studies, and Gender Studies before they graduate from UC San Diego.

- We demand the programs and departments such as OASIS, Campus Community Centers, Ethnic Studies, Critical Gender Studies, CLAH, and African American Studies Minor amongst others continue to have solid funding for the work they do in retaining African American students and educating the campus as a whole.
- We demand the University implements, maintains and fully funds BSU's Student Initiated Yield Programs. Stipend for Student Volunteers- students deserves compensation for the hard work they do that the University should be doing.
- We demand that the Chancellor's Office offers more campus-wide support for the African-American students on this campus, as well as the other historically underrepresented and under-served communities on this campus.
- We demand the University provide the African-American community with a temporary location for a safe space on campus while the African-American Resource Center is being planned and constructed.
- We demand the University provide free tutors for the African-American students who seek academic support. This can be structured similar to that of the Athletic Department's services to Athletes.
- We demand a response!

THE ISSUE

As you may or may not be aware of the recent events that occurred involving some UC San Diego undergraduate students in an attempt to make a mockery of Black History month and host a themed party entitled "The Compton Cookout". This is completely unacceptable. The University has made two meager attempts to alleviate the tension between the UCSD community and spread awareness to the population but that those attempts have been to no avail. Our question and major concern is how does a student/group of students feel that it is acceptable to target a group of color. This issue is a direct reflection of the insensitivity on this campus and has acted as a catalyst in this already existing hostile environment. This address is to not focus on the event specifically but to 1) use this situation as a learning experience for everyone who may or may not have been affected 2) hold the Chancellor and the University accountable to making campus climate a priority and addressing the needs of the African-American community and historically underrepresented ethnic communities on this campus. The administration's failure to prioritize creating a healthier campus climate earlier has caused this tragic event to reach the masses. It needs to be addressed immediately and all members involved in the organizing of the racist event should face dire consequences. The University needs to make an example out of these students.

Earlier this year the Black Student Union, with the help of a larger statewide coalition, organized and coordinated the Do UC us? Campaign in an effort to increase the numbers of African-American students on the UC San Diego campus. The campaign also clearly addressed the issues of campus climate at this University compiled with Admissions Statistics and criteria, Diversity and Yield Reports from the University as well as student testimonies, demands and student initiated programs to increase the yield of African American students. The UCSD Vice Chancellor of Student Affairs, Penny Rue, has committed to fully funding the yield programs and through this public address along with support we will surely hold her accountable to that. Consequently, with the media involved, this issue has reached national attention and has sadly marked UCSD to be a "racist campus". This is completely problematic because this incident is pushing us back in our efforts of access, yield and retention. Students have been working countless hours developing yield programs for the black students that will succeed but now more ever we are conflicted. We want to increase the numbers of African-American students on this campus but we do not want them to experience the hostile environment that we have to deal with.

WHAT WE HAVE DONE

What type of campus climate do we have at this University that would allow this type of behavior/ activity to be acceptable?

This incident has given us a moral edge.

The Black Student Union will continuously represent the voice of the African-American student population and raise issues regarding campus climate because we are confident that an inclusive campus climate fosters higher retention rates, student development, and academic empowerment. BSU requests that you all review the needs and that we schedule a quarterly meeting to update, assess, and evaluate.

The Black Student Union has been in existence on this campus since 1968. We are apart of the history of UCSD! African-American students have made instrumental steps for pushing for social justice and equality for all students on campus for decades. The University is planning its 50 Year Celebration and in that half century our population of African American students has never exceeded 3%. The campus having never seen a black population of over 3 percent speaks to the lack of initiative and prioritization of yield and diversity outreach. Students on this campus that make continual efforts to undermine the history of oppression of African-Americans in this country and the racism and bigotry we have surmounted.

HISTORY/SUPPORT

To our fellow students, lets take care of each other. We have to continue to push through the hardship that this situation has caused us and use it as a blessing in disguise. We WILL stay united and our community will hold the University accountable to prioritizing a healthier campus climate for underrepresented groups on this campus. To our extremely supportive faculty and staff, thank you and please continue to push, encourage and guide us as student leaders and activist. To Chancellor Fox, Vice Chancellor Rue and the rest of University Administration, we demand you commit to the UCSD "Principles of Community".

STEPS FOR THE FUTURE: UPCOMING MEETINGS

Monday Feb 22nd 6:30—BSU general body meeting in Cross Cultural Center in the Comunidad Room

Tuesday Feb 23rd 5–7pm—"Honest and Open Dialogue on Campus Climate"- Muir Quad, Facilitated by Fnann Keflezighi

Wednesday Feb 24th 12–2pm Teach-ins and 2–4pm Open Dialogue-facilitated by Briana Boyd-Price Center Ballroom East

Thursday Feb 25th 4:30–6:30pm—Campus Black Forum (CBF)— Cross Cultural Center library (please note that CBF is a space created for the African American community and you may or may not be welcomed into this space especially in this time of pain)

The University Administration should feel embarrassed for allowing such negligence to occur. We warned the University about the hostile environment for Black students within this horrible campus climate. Other students of underrepresented groups share the same dismay.

It is imperative that our African-American community reaches a critical mass on this campus.

We are committed to fulfilling our vision of a healthier campus climate in order to continue our work in the struggle to recruit, yield, retain and most importantly represent the African American students here at UC San Diego.

David Ritcherson
Fnann Keflezighi
Chairpersons of the Black Student Union

Photo courtesy of Erik Jepsen.

UCSD Teach-In Address
Performance is Not Benign
Dr. Nadine George-Graves
Associate Professor, Theater and Dance
February 24, 2010

Good afternoon.

My name is Nadine George-Graves and I'm an Associate Professor here in the Department of Theater and Dance. I have devoted my entire professional life and scholarship to issues of race and gender in performance. Here are some classes that I have taught here:

- African American Theater
- African American Film
- Gender and Performance
- The Body and Performance
- Ethnicity and Performativity

My books are:

- *The Royalty of Negro Vaudeville: The Whitman Sisters and the Negotiations of Race, Gender, and Class in African American Theater, 1900-1940*

and the forthcoming

- *Urban Bush Women: Twenty Years of African American Dance Theater, Community Engagement, and Working It Out*

I have many articles on similar topics and my creative work as a director also deals with these issues. I say this because I know there has been some backlash against this event and wonder if the speakers are qualified to talk on the subject. So I wanted to let you know where I'm coming from as a scholar.

I want to start off by saying that I fully support the BSU students and faculty of African descent in their efforts to bring about real structural change that has been an ongoing struggle escalated by recent events. I want to acknowledge the strong responses against these acts from many different constituents in our community, not just African Americans, who stand in solidarity with these efforts.

A number of students in the department of Theater and Dance have written a statement that begins to get at some of these issues from a perspective that has not been fully addressed in the blogs and open letters that I've read so far. We're passing them out today and will post it online. I encourage you to read it because I can only give a nod to these issues here. This is not an official statement from the department of Theater and Dance, doesn't represent everyone in that department's opinion but the students felt strongly that they wanted to get this word out to you and add their voices to the many others decrying the actions and calling for institutional change and I support them in that. We are also passing out a statement from the department chair. I encourage you to read the blogs on stopracismucsd.wordpress.com as well as the battlehate.ucsd.edu website. I encourage you to read as much as you can—talk to as many people as you can and educate yourselves, because I can't do it all in 15 minutes. I encourage you to take classes that address these issues especially if you don't see anything wrong with these events.

I've been asked to explain the historical and social context surrounding the "Compton Cookout" to help people understand why the originating incident is "a big deal." I'll be honest with you, when first asked, I was concerned, ambivalent and a bit outraged about this charge. My entire body of scholarship is dedicated to analyzing and articulating the negotiations of power in terms of race, class and gender through performance on and off stage. So it makes sense that I was asked. But how do I condense that rich and complex scholarship into 15 minutes? But as events escalated I decided that I wanted to use this opportunity to do a small part toward battling ignorance.

Of course, two hours is a drop in the bucket. And this must be part of the larger response from the University and not just a band-aid. We must all keep the administration accountable for that.

I can't tell you how many versions of this talk I've written, each in response to the latest occurrence or internet response or news piece. And I stand here right now, not quite knowing what to say. This has become so enflamed that I seriously doubt anybody can hear what I have to say.

- There is no trust on this campus
- The atmosphere is toxic and hostile.
- The atmosphere was toxic and hostile before but it has become unbearable and unsustainable.
- This community has fractured.

Unless the demographics of student, staff and faculty representation and the commitment to work in areas of race, ethnicity, gender, class, disability and cognate fields is more fully supported, nothing I can say here today will matter.

Not to mention this is just plain embarrassing. UCSD is becoming known nationally as an institution of intolerance and ignorance. What year is this?! I hope the university takes quick, decisive and sufficient measures to address the campus climate, starting with the already existing yield report and the calls for action from the students who are bravely leading us all. I hope we all commit to our part of the project of ensuring that something like this doesn't happen again. And I hope that we can all commit to our part in changing the atmosphere so that students don't think these behaviors are sanctioned. Because I don't know how much longer I can take it and I'm sure there are others of you who agree.

So, what do I do? Do I try to begin to talk about these issues or do I stop here and give up?

I'm not one to give up, so I'll try to do my small part.

My other area of concern was who to address. The students who threw and attended this party? The students who are the target of these vicious representations and have to live with the fallout? The faculty and administration members who have fostered the toxic campus environment that allows students to think this event was harmless?

What I've decided to do is to begin with the premise that these events and others like them are wrong and that they instill hatred, racism and violence. If you don't believe me then I refer you to the library; or to the many responses that have come from various departments and faculty members who study this stuff; or to this huge national outcry denouncing the actions.

I've decided to address this talk to those of you in the room who know that this incident was wrong (no matter what your race, class, gender or age) but don't quite know how to articulate your feelings when talking to roommates or colleagues who pose different beliefs and ask certain questions. There are many ways to approach this but I want to show you how the language of theater studies and performance studies is particularly useful for understanding the events and fallout.

So the title of the talk is Performance is Not Benign.

I'm currently teaching a class on the body in performance and my students and I discussed this at length and some of this talk comes from those discussions.

The imagery described in the original party invitation draws on a long history of stereotyping first begun in the theater genre of minstrelsy in the early 1800s. Minstrelsy has the dubious distinction of being labeled the first truly American theater form. Prior to minstrelsy's inception, American audiences were entertained by versions of music hall and variety that were imported from England albeit with an American flair. But minstrelsy is all ours and as such has become one of the primary narratives of human interaction in this country. And the development of stereotypical character types is the most significant legacy of minstrelsy. These types were developed not only to ridicule and entertain; they also served very significant social functions. As popular culture, minstrelsy marked changing social tide and served as a site for racial negotiation during antebellum, wartime and reconstruction. Minstrelsy was a performative argument for slavery. It presented African Americans as less than human and therefore only worthy of being slaves. And it has resurfaced over and over again throughout American history. It was used as the argument for Jim Crow laws and the continued second-class citizenship of African Americans, among many other directly destructive effects. So that as the times changed, the stereotypes changed but they always served to disenfranchise African Americans, even when African Americans do it. Because we are all implicated in these narratives. There is a complicated history of African Americans also performing these roles but that happening doesn't diminish the negative power of the stereotypes and it remains with us as a constant anxious negotiation of classed, raced and gendered bodies with different particulars but doing the same cultural work.

The original party invitation acts as a script. And the event itself was a rehearsal of the negotiation of power. It gives people the performative argument for the continued systematic oppression of poor, black and brown men and women. In other words, by playing at mocking a group of people one can practice not respecting them as human beings. We can tell ourselves it is all done in fun but it fundamentally changes the way we see those people in the future especially at a place like this when there are so few of us that you see. This is not just symptomatic of racism but it creates racism—it enacts racism again and again. There are many reasons why—just one of which is the fact that this was a mockery of black history month. And the social work of this party will come back to haunt other spaces—job interviews, legislative chambers with lawmakers drafting legislation, doctor's offices, classrooms—this is where racial profiling comes from.

Performance is Not Benign.

I could go on and point to other moments in history where these kinds of acts were negotiated. But what I thought would be most useful is to focus on developing language to help us articulate our feelings of dissent. I've talked to a number of people who essentially say, "I know it was wrong but I don't quite know how to respond when somebody says____." I want to use the time I have left to talk about some of the more complicated conversations that people have had and start us sharing strategies for how to respond. So, I'd like you to think about one such moment that has happened to you in the past week. When you didn't know what to say when confronted about your beliefs. Turn to your neighbor, introduce yourself if you don't know the person and explain the situation, what you did or didn't do or say, and try to work together to come up with a way to respond.

I'll start you off with an example: Somebody said to me "People are so sensitive. It doesn't mean anything and I'm tired of people complaining." To which I said, "Well let's talk about this oppression fatigue—who gets the right to be bored, who gets the right to dictate who is offended? I was to resist allowing others to dictate the terms of my offense and I'm bored with people who are bored with the continued acts of racism. If these acts didn't persist, if we didn't have an atmosphere that fed the ignorance then we wouldn't have these problems and we could all get on with our lives. But they do persist, it is important and people don't feel safe, so we can't stop."

Another comment was "I don't want to look stupid so I don't say anything." To which I responded, "Well how can we create a climate of respect especially in this educational setting so that you can feel comfortable working through these issues."

Those are just a few examples.

So take a few minutes to do that—turn to your neighbor and talk about a situation you experienced and what you said or wish you had said.

(After a few minutes…)

I'm out of time but I hope this has gone a little way in our productive conversations. I invite you to bring up those situations when we open up the discussion so that we can all think together of strategies for battling racism, sexism, classism and homophobia.

Thank you.

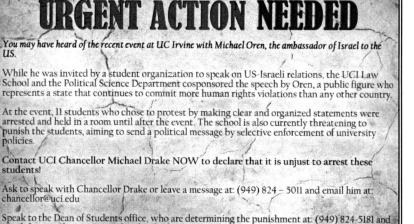

URGENT ACTION NEEDED

You may have heard of the recent event at UC Irvine with Michael Oren, the ambassador of Israel to the US.

While he was invited by a student organization to speak on US-Israeli relations, the UCI Law School and the Political Science Department cosponsored the speech by Oren, a public figure who represents a state that continues to commit more human rights violations than any other country.

At the event, 11 students who chose to protest by making clear and organized statements were arrested and held in a room until after the event. The school is also currently threatening to punish the students, aiming to send a political message by selective enforcement of university policies.

Contact UCI Chancellor Michael Drake NOW to declare that it is unjust to arrest these students!

Ask to speak with Chancellor Drake or leave a message at: (949) 824 – 5011 and email him at: chancellor@uci.edu

Speak to the Dean of Students office, who are determining the punishment at: (949) 824-5181 and email them at: deanstu@uci.eduivil rights movement in America the eventually ensured equality and human rights for all minorities.

Thank you for your support. **www.irvine11.com**

JENN TRAN ANNOUNCES ASIAN AMERICAN/ASIAN PACIFIC ISLANDER TOWN HALL MEETING

Outside the Chancellor's office, March 1, 2010

My name is Jenn Tran and I'm a fifth year at UCSD. I represent Ethnic Studies and Urban Planning, and I think that one thing that needs to be mentioned is … if any of you all were at the teach-in/teach-out, one of the things that Nadine George reminded me is that "who are we speaking to?"

And one thing that touched me is that she said we're speaking to the people who say "why does this matter?" *Why does this matter?* And everyone here obviously knows that this is important to all of y'all, but that is why I say that there's a lot of people out there that still don't know why this matters right now. And that is why our job is to continue not only being in solidarity with one another right now, getting to know each other, connecting, going back to the roots of where we all come from, but as an Asian American I want to also reiterate that we are a major minority, not only on this campus but UC-wide, and in higher education, and we need to keep all of us accountable for what's happening.

So tomorrow night at the Cross Cultural Center, Ethnic Studies and Literature professors are inviting all Asian American and A/PI students and other UC orgs to come to say, to speak on, you know, *why does this matter* — to all students, but in particular to Asian American students in this issue that's going around. So I invite you tomorrow night, at the Cross Cultural Center, from 7-9:00 p.m. … There's also a Facebook statement that's been circulating, and there's a petition as well, and so, you know, if you can't make it, sign it, and be in solidarity with the BSU right now.

Thank you.

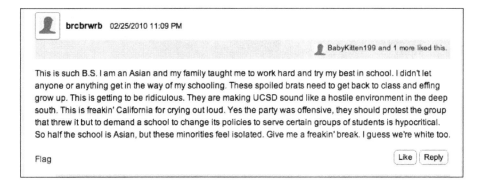

brcbrwrb   02/25/2010 11:09 PM

BabyKitten199 and 1 more liked this.

This is such B.S. I am an Asian and my family taught me to work hard and try my best in school. I didn't let anyone or anything get in the way of my schooling. These spoiled brats need to get back to class and effing grow up. This is getting to be ridiculous. They are making UCSD sound like a hostile environment in the deep south. This is freakin' California for crying out loud. Yes the party was offensive, they should protest the group that threw it but to demand a school to change its policies to serve certain groups of students is hypocritical. So half the school is Asian, but these minorities feel isolated. Give me a freakin' break. I guess we're white too.

Flag

Like   Reply

MY LIFE BELONGS TO THE STUDENTS

Cecilia Ubilla, Summer Bridge Writing Coordinator, UCSD OASIS program, Library Walk, Friday after the noose, February 26, 2010

I have been on this campus for 30 years. And I have been on this struggle since I was in high school like the compañeras and compañitos from Lincoln High school that were here. I've seen much injustice and I have suffered much on my own person. I have cried days and nights in other places in the world and here.

I came here in 1974 as a graduate student and this university welcomed me. And then I found a family and professors who are still here, who are human, who respect peoples' dignity. And I felt that I had found a real warm, a real humane place. But in 30 years that paradise is somewhat turning into a nightmare from which I run away. I have seen much mobilization on this campus. Because they cut the trees. Because they didn't cut the trees. Because they opened ground for this, they didn't open up ground for that. Every issue I have been here. Not for me, not for my colleagues who are here with me today, not for the professors, but for the students. Because that is the objective of my life. And it will always be.

It is time to dry the tears. It is time to take action. We have suffered. No one probably on this campus has suffered more than the African American students because history has oppressed them throughout their entire existence. I did see their pain in Austin, Texas, and the entire state of Texas in the 60s, when horrible things like this happened and nobody did anything. I think that the students on this campus are so committed to their studies, so committed to the library and the lab, that they have missed the point, they have gotten out of history

Photo courtesy of Erik Jepsen.

and we need to bring them back. They need to know there is an enemy and these things do not happen by accident. I'm here with you, and as I've always said, I offer my life, and my life belongs to the students. Twice in my life I came very close to losing it; and if I need to lose it now, so be it, it's yours.

I think that educating yourself is very good. Educating this crowd is very good. But I think there is a crowd on this campus that is a mainstream American crowd that have never studied their history and they've never come to terms with how they belong to the enemy and how they are part of the repressive apparatus of this nation. We need to educate them!

Madame Chancellor, about 2 months ago, I received from your hands a medal, because I have been here serving the students for over 30 years. You cannot imagine how happy that medal made me. Not for me, but because it reminded me of my father. An uneducated guy who said to me, in his lack of literacy at all, that the only thing that I could get in life and win was an education.

Please help me to continue to love that medal, Madame Chancellor, and please tell the students that you understand better than anyone else, that in spite of all the pressures that we know you're under, that you will expel some fraternities from this campus. And even if the people make an issue, get the *Koala* out of this campus. If it's a violation of civil liberities, then I would say, civil liberties that attack and degenerate the dignity, the pride, and the freedom of human beings to do what they want to do, for their own dignity, are not laws to be respected.

High School Students from the African Revolutionary Student Organization, Lincoln High School, San Diego, CA

Friday morning rally after the noose was found, February 26, 2010

Marquel Carnell: ... I know there is the rage of 1200 black and brown students here, but there's more than that, there's the rage of a whole community here against the selfishness, the racism, and the bigotry that has occurred here, and I hope you guys know that we're with you all the way, right behind you!

Sakeenah Shabazz: I'm Sakeenah Shabazz, a junior at Lincoln high school, and I'm up here representing ARSO, the African Revolutionary Student Organization, and the fact that Marquel is able to come up here and eloquently express the rage that he feels, is so tight, because we are the products of the Lincoln High School Center for Social Justice, and this is the stuff that we're learning about. And seeing that it's right here in front of us, and that it's real, it kinda hurts our hearts to know, but it just shows that

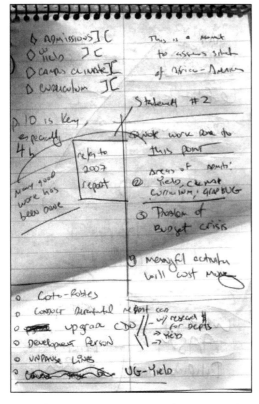

we have to get out here and make a change, because if you don't do anything, ain't nothing gonna happen. And it's good to see there's a lot of diverse faces out here... [*crowd cheers drown out speaker*]..we'd like to be out here together, and be with you guys, but we're taking care of our grades. We will be the college students in 2, 3, 4 years, you know, so it's very important that we stand alongside you guys. Because if we don't fight for it, who is? And if you guys don't fight for it, how is our education in the future going to be any better than it is right now? So it's good that we're out here struggling together, and it's, **it's gonna happen, whether that chancellor likes it or not**, so...." [*and the crowd goes wild}*

Jose Navarro, MAAC Community School Senior, Chula Vista, CA

Student-led Teach-Out, February 24, 2010

Wow! That's a lot of people! (laughs) Alright, first of all the mustache may fool you, but I am 19. I am a senior at the MAAC community charter down in Chula Vista, down in the south bay. A couple of years ago, immigration was really crazy, we walked out of our schools like you walked out of yours. This ends today! I have seen my father get deported because of his race, and now the police look at me.

And I'm going to stand today, in front of this university, and tell them: I am not going to come to this school if you can not protect me from racist people in this world.

I come from a school of 300 people and every one of them have written to the UCSD chancellor to let them know we are not going to stand for this, you are not going to stand for this. Latinos and blacks need to stand together!

One thing I've noticed from every person who is in power: they hate people who fight power. If you fight back, change will come. That teach-in, in there, was nothing. This, right now, is something you have to SHOW. No one will hear you unless you knock on the door! Knock that door down, let it be known that we are not going to stand for this!

I was here yesterday—I love this campus, I like it, don't get me wrong … but I can't be in a place where I know I won't be safe … I'm big enough to protect myself, but what about the ones who can not be protected? What about the ones who have no voice? What about the ones who stand there and don't know what to say, or how to say it?

So when I leave right now, MAAC students, students from the South Bay, students from the Latino community, will always be here to stand behind you no matter what. I was always taught to stand up for what is right—even teachers I argue with will tell you that.

I've been in every situation—pulled over by Border Patrol just because they see the color of my skin and because I have a big mustache like my dad—I've been told "you are not going to be anything more than a gangbanger, or selling drugs, or doing something."

I'm standing here today, to look you in the face, and to say "I'M CHANGING MY WORLD!!"

Minorities should not be looking to the school to "boost their numbers". They should be doing that themselves by: getting better grades in high school; taking college preparatory classes, Advanced Placement or Honors classes, scoring higher on the SAT and ACT; even actually applying to the University. The party was in poor taste but it was mocking a particular sub sect of inner city life that minorities should be trying to rid themselves of rather than yelling at people who point out their flaws. White people make fun of "rednecks", "crackers", "hillbillies" and "white trash". And so do black people. But we don't hold press conferences and rallies over insults directed at the morons of our race so grow some thicker skin and don't behave in a way that would confuse people about your personal character.
WorkingCitizen (02/25/2010, 7:21 AM)

Report Comment

Photo courtesy of Erik Jepsen.

A Moment of Silence for the Kumeyaay Tribe

Aries Yumul, Friday morning rally after the noose, February 26, 2010

I just want to ask if we can all take a moment of silence right now.
Because the land that we're on is actually a burial ground for the
Kumeyaay Tribe.
So if we can just take a moment, please, to recognize that …

Cookout Uncovers Need for Structural Change

The Guardian *UCSD student paper, February 22, 2010*

Dear Editor,

We submit that the so-called "Compton Cookout" incident has less to do with the racist culture of a particular fraternity or the Greek system in general (although that is certainly a factor) than it does with long-standing structural problems at UCSD—lack of a critical mass of faculty and students of color, generic (specific, community-neutral) approaches to improving campus climate, a very low profile and poorly funded African-American and Chicano studies curricular programs, etc. Together all of these institutional weaknesses produce a campus climate that emboldens the kind of racism we saw in the language and proposed activities of the "Compton Cookout."

We urge the administration to avoid psychological interpretations of the incident. Individual behavior and attitudes are not the primary source of the problem. It will not be enough to oppose racist speech with "more speech," with lessons about the limits of satire or even with well intentioned but ultimately symbolic campaigns such as the proposed "Not in Our Community" initiative.

This incident, and the potential for others in the future, should convince campus policymakers that serious structural changes are long overdue. In our opinion, the administration should take immediate action

and 1) commit to permanent and substant
and staffing for the African American S
2) establish an Organized Research Unit
research on local communities of color that
represented at UCSD, 3) create a task force to
the desirability of rotating public art installatio.
linked to underrepresented minority communities (pref-
erably local) and 4) reorganize the office of the Chief
Diversity Officer in order to facilitate the writing of
a campuswide plan for addressing campus climate with a
focus on how climate affects specific groups.

We understand that in a time of budgetary constraints,
some of these proposed solutions will be difficult
to implement. And yet these kinds of changes ought
to receive the highest priority if we are to believe
Chancellor Marye Anne Fox when she says the campus has
a serious commitment to diversity. What is undeniable
is that UCSD must change what it has been doing on the
diversity front up until now. It's simply not working.

—Jorge Mariscal
Professor, Literature Department

—Patrick Velasquez
Director, Office of Academic Support and Instructional
Services

Thoughts at the Asian American/Asian Pacific Islander Town Hall Meeting

Professor Tak Fujitani, History, March 2, 2010

Hello everybody! I've missed the most exciting week in 17 years! I've been here for 17 years, but I was giving a lecture in London—on RACISM!!! ... I couldn't ever imagine, in the past, wanting to hurry up and come back to my workplace. But this week, it's different, it's historic!

Growing up, everybody asked me where I was from, because my name is Takashi, right? And I would say, "I'm from California! Where are you from!?" I grew up in California, I went to only public schools in California, I went through the entire University of California, I am the beneficiary of public education in California. And that's why I have been so concerned about the resegregation of education in California. Many of the people in here were involved for so many years in establishing departments, programs, other unofficial organizations that were dedicated to fighting racism and opening up the university for everybody.

There was an organization in the mid-90's that I remember very fondly, called the Coalition Against Segregation in Education. Unfortunately, we didn't succeed! (laughter) You know, in the short run. But I think what we have seen over this last week or so is the fruition of all the hard work that has been done by so many people across a broad coalition. It's not limited to one group or another, it's about coalition-building, and that's why its beautiful to see so many different people in this room, so many different people across all the town meetings, across all the big demonstrations that we have had, in my absence! (crowd laughs)

Anyway, I'm here! I'm ready to act! There's more to come, right?

But one of the things that I really want to say—I took this up with my class, I'm teaching a class on the second World War in the Asian

Pacific—one of my students said, "Professor, why are we talking about race so much? Why can't we have a normal class?" So I had to say, "What is normal? What is normality?" Unfortunately, the normal is that in this university, and in most places, is usually that we don't talk about race, we don't confront it, we just make the assumption that we're past racism. So students are used to that. They want to just know a history of the war which is about battleships, or whatever. I never talk about those things. But I do talk about race!

One of the other questions that my students raised with me the other day, because it's disproportionately Asian, they say "What does racism have to do with us, in a situation where there are so many of us here?" And my response to that is remember—it's ironic, but racism doesn't recognize any particular color line. Because it's gonna start here, and it's gonna move on, and one day, when you think you "made it," it's going to hit you. So that's why we need to be careful about it. And it's not just about color, either. That's why racism really intersects, as other people have been saying, with sexism, with classism, it's all the same system, to keep us down and to divide us. So that's one really important thing to think about.

But another, why should Asians be concerned about racism against black people, or others? What I have to say about that is that we have to also remember that WE are now in positions of privilege. Somehow, we have made it. It's not only about us, right? If people only thought about, you know, "I'm happy now, and therefore everything is good," the world is never going to be a better place. We have—you have—WE have a certain obligation to keep up the struggle so that the university is a more open, equal, non-racist place!

If I was a Christian—which I am not—I would want to say, "If you don't get involved, you might go to hell!" (loud laughter) But I don't know that to be true! But I DO know, that if you do get involved, you're going to feel a whole lot better about yourself, you're going to feel a whole lot better about the world, and the world is going to get better!

Professor Dennis Childs, Literature, Speaks at Teach-Out

February 24, 2010

First of all, I want to say that I'm proud to come up here after people like Dr. Weber, and I'm proud to come up here after Dr. Edwina Welch. I tell people this over and over again. I'm in my third year teaching at this university, I teach in the Literature Department. Many of you out here have been in my classes, many of you I've worked with in a variety of faculties on this campus. And I would not be able to survive here without the Cross Cultural Center and the work she does and the staff of that center do. And I know that a lot of you share that experience. Their leadership role on campus would not be possible were it not for the leadership role of the students that we have before you today. So, I wanna say as someone put into a role as a leader and as someone who councils young people as a professor and as a member of the community in San Diego, I'm taking leadership cues from you, the students. Particularly those students involved in organizations like the BSU. And like MEChA. I can say without a shadow of doubt that I would not be able to survive as a faculty of color, and particularly a black male faculty on this campus, which if you haven't recognized, we're also a very very very small number on this campus. And in terms of that leadership role that organizations such as MEChA and BSU play on this campus, I wanna say, it started way before this event.

About a week or so before all this crisis erupted, or at least it became obvious to some people that it was a crisis, a lot of people knew about this crisis ever since they set foot on this campus. But at least a week before this iteration of the crisis happened, I was invited by BSU and MEChA to speak at a high school day for local high school students of African and Latino descent. And they brought up, what was it, 600 high school students from local schools. Brown, black and Asian students from local schools to this campus, that for them seems like an alien territory. I spoke to the black students particularly that day. And when I talked to them, I didn't try to sugarcoat the reality that a lot of us face on this campus. And

I looked out into those eyes, and I wasn't being a cheerleader for UCSD, I wanted to let them know that someone like me is here should they decide to come here. But in letting them know that, while I was speaking right here in the east ballroom of the Price Center, I had a pain in my chest. Because I knew as I was looking into that crowd, particularly at somebody like a young black male from the high school I went to. I from San Diego. I went to Hoover High School in City Heights (*crowd cheering very loudly*). This is not a joke to me. So when people talk about real pain, this is a pain that I have experienced on a personal level and my family has experienced on a personal level for YEARS in this community. There's a reason why we called San Diego "Klan Diego" when I went to high school. And its not because of *individual* racist people. Dr. Mariscal, all the students, everybody who has been speaking has been talking about this is not about individual racist people. *This is about a white supremacist, classist, sexist, misogynistic institution! And homophobic*! (*crowd going wild*)

We cannot mistake the skin color of who enacts a white supremacist act for it being not white supremacist, in case it's a black person. I know that sounds a little convoluted so I'll repeat it: It doesn't matter whether black people went to this party! It matters that the party itself represents a structural problem on this campus, and in this country. And that pain that I had in my chest when I was speaking to those hundreds of youth, who have goals and dreams, and realities that a lot of people can't understand, even in San Diego county, coming from a place like City Heights, you are taught from the very jump that this space right here doesn't belong to you. It is ingrained in you like the air you breathe and the water you drink. *None of them* feel like this is their space! And so when I'm looking into the faces of kids like that, they are very very aware of how white supremacy acts in the world. They didn't *need* the Compton cookout to be told that UCSD is racist.

So my students know I like to throw out statistics. And so this pain in my chest that im talking about, when I look at that black male or that Latino male at the high school conference, and know that there's 40 percent Latino population in the california prison system, 9 percent here at UCSD. 30 percent African American population in prison system, 1.3 at UCSD.

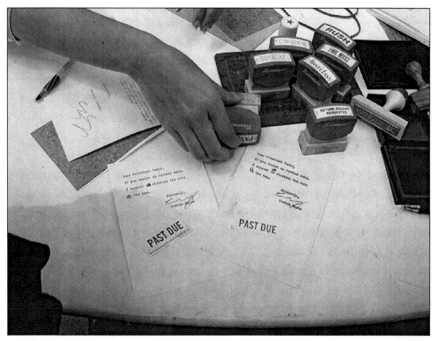

Photo courtesy of Curtis Marez.

Now you do the math. They *know* where they're being trained to go. Their schools look more like prisons than schools! So you statisticians out there, I want you to keep this in your back pocket, and keep it there and say something about it. 5 to 1, 5 to 1 is the ratio of black males in this state cages to colleges. 5 to 1 is the ratio of blacks men in cages to colleges in this beautiful multicultural society that we live in; and this university and every university in the state, is implicated in that statistic. We all have to put that at the front of the work we're doing. So when you talk about diversity, and talk about outreach and all these things, you wanna talk about a state of emergency? The state of emergency is endemic to this place, and in terms of the leadership role that BSU has played, I want *everybody* to look at the demands they've made of this university. Everybody should have a copy of that and everybody, no matter where you're coming from, no matter what race, socioeconomic background, sexuality—should stand behind BSU on all those demands. *Including* the repatriation of the ancestral remains! (*wild cheering*). So when I talk to a young man or a young woman because we can't forget that the highest percentage increase in demographic in the prison system in this state is women of color. Latinas and black women particularly. So when I look at those statistics, relative to the statistics of faculty, staff and students on this campus, that's where the pain comes for me. It was there before this event, and it will be there until we smash the system that dictated this event.

So I wanna extend my heartfelt thanks to everyone who is sitting here today. And particularly I wanna extend my heartfelt thanks and love to the overall community of people of color and allies on this campus. And most particularly I wanna extend my love and support and honor to the work of people like Fnann and David at BSU. And all the other members of BSU and allied organizations. Like Mar Velez, another student of mine.

So we are gonna hold the faculty of this university and the black faculty of this university in particular, are gonna hold this university accountable along with the students. We have issued a letter that I hope all of you read. And we're also going to issue some..."recommendations", whatever we want to call them, I call them *demands* because I cannot work here in good conscience and stay here and be used as a token by this university ...

Thank you very much, and keep on fighting!

SORTING THROUGH RACE RELATIONS AT UCSD

Excerpted from KPBS program, "These Days." Maureen Cavanaugh hosts a discussion with UC San Diego Prof. Sara Clarke Kaplan, Andrea Guerrero (ACLU), and Glynda Davis, UC San Diego Assistant Chancellor of Diversity. Originally broadcast February 25, 2010.

CAVANAUGH: Let me ask you, Sara, because you teach Ethnic and Gender Studies at UCSD. Tell us your reaction, if you would. I don't even know how to phrase the question right now. Just tell us your reaction to not only the party but also what's happened on campus this week.

KAPLAN: Absolutely. And I just want to clarify one thing and, Glynda, correct me if I'm wrong. But I actually believe that UCSD's admission rate of African-American students is, in general, according to the 2006 Yield Report, about on par with some of the other top UCs. The problem I think that UCSD has is not one of admission but one of acceptance, and that's the sort of question of yield. It's not that students—that there aren't tons of very qualified if not over qualified young African-American students who are being accepted to UCSD, about at the same rates as at Berkeley or UCLA, it's that we actually can't seem to get them to come.

CAVANAUGH: Exactly. I read a statistic where there's about a 13% acceptance rate among black, qualified black students who are accepted to UCSD, as opposed to about 44% up at UCLA.

KAPLAN: Absolutely.

CAVANAUGH: So what's—why is that?

KAPLAN: Well, and I think, you know, this is interesting, Maureen. I haven't been on KPBS for a year, on *These Days* for a year, and the last time I was here we were talking about Black History Month, and we were talking about whether there's still a need for Black History Month post Obama. And at the time, I said I think that, of course, you know, I do still believe in Black History Month but I think the bigger question is not Black History Month but what does it mean that we don't learn the history of African-Americans and other people of color in the United States the other months of the year outside of the classrooms like Ethnic Studies, outside of the classrooms like African-American Studies. If this was, in fact, part of what we think about as part of what makes up America every day, we wouldn't need Black History Month. And I guess I would say about both the student reaction on campus and I think, more broadly, the faculty reaction and staff reaction is that like Black History Month, this is not about the Compton Cookout. The problem is not that the Compton Cookout happened, though that is a problem, or even that the Koala then used campus resources and campus television to directly violate the code of conduct and principles of community, I think the broader problem is that we have a longstanding campus climate which the students, faculty and administration have been well aware of for at least, you know, this administration since Chancellor Fox, with all due respect, came into the position, that has yet to be fixed. And that the incredible sense of hostility and alienation toward African-American students and other students of color is what made this kind of event permissible. So when we say how could this happen? How could they think this is okay, I think honestly as teachers and as administrators, we have to look at ourselves and say they think it's okay because we have not created an educational climate that tells them that it's not... .

While I may disagree with the concept behind the party, the students have the right to hold it as long as it wasn%u2019t on campus. I want to know how they know how many Caucasian, Hispanic or Blacks attend the college? Or why does the school allow a Black Student Union? The NAACP and Affirmative Action are exactly the same as the KKK. Programs to support racism! Ask yourself why the US Census needs to know your race, or why organizations exist only to support a single race or idea.
METANAME (02/25/2010, 5:58 PM)

Report Comment

CAVANAUGH: Right, right...Sara, let me come to you. You know, several years ago when the UC Regents basically said no more affirmative action policies, you know, across these campuses, we were basically kind of told that we were in a different world now, that the playing field was if not equal at least more level than it ever had been. And yet we see this problem with diversity not only at UCSD but on campuses throughout California. So what happened?

KAPLAN: I think that's a question that we're all constantly trying to figure out. And I think that, you know, there've been many studies and there are some things that we know what happened. We know that, for example, that the guarantee of admission for the top 4% actually doesn't take into account the fact that fourth and fifth quintile schools offer different courses which means that the GPAs of those students look very, very different, right? Because students get extra credit for taking APs, they get extra credit for honors, and so when you're in low income schools, which tend to have higher representations of historically under-represented minorities, what you will see is that they simply don't have access to those kinds of classes, that there are many, many schools in the state of California where you can't take the basic requirements you need to take to get into a UC. You actually cannot even apply. In fact, you can't even apply to a Cal State with what they offer. You have to go to community college and transfer. And those, again, traditionally are schools with low income students and students of color. I think also what we have to recognize is that what we saw with Proposition 209, what we saw with Proposition 227, what we saw with Proposition 187 was, in fact, I think less of a claim that we were in a post-racial state and more a profound backlash by voters in the state of California against the perceived increased access and visibility of people of color in the state of California, anxieties about it becoming a majority-minority state and that rather than that being a sort of moment of propositional politics that said oh, few were done, I actually think it was a moment of profound racial backlash against people of color and their success and that's why it had precisely the result you would imagine it had.

CAVANAUGH: And you would argue … argue it had that ripple effect … even down to admissions at UCSD.

KAPLAN: And particularly, I think, down to campus climate. If you go online right now, you can find a Facebook group of students of color and white students, not just——and I say this because I want it to be clear it's not just white students saying that African-American students want a free ride, saying that they don't work hard, saying that the reason that there aren't more black students at UCSD or the other UCs is because, you know, they're just not qualified to get in. So, clearly, there's a problem… And, unfortunately, what I've seen over the last ten years since the dismantling of affirmative action is that universities used affirmative action as a crutch. They did not use it as the cast to heal the broken leg. They used it as the excuse for not doing anything else. Well, now we don't have that excuse. There is absolutely no excuse for the university not to fix the structural inequities that exist in the admissions process, in the recruitment process, in the outreach process, in their curricular offerings process, in the faculty hiring process… And so I think at a certain point we have to ask where the administrative commitment is. I look at these students and I think, in fact, it's easy for us as faculty or administrators or staff to say, oh, we do this work. But the fact is we do about a tenth of the work. The students at UCSD are doing 90% of the work to recruit and retain to make access for others on that campus, and they're doing it for free and they're doing it instead of studying. And that's our failure as teachers and faculty.

For a culture that has the second lowest high school graduation rate in the country (Latinos have the lowest) they sure make a lot of noise. This country has bent over backwards to accommodate African Americans. "Black History Month"? Give me a break. Racism isn't going to end until people stop using it to get something given to them. To paraphrase Bill Cosby "Stop whining and work harder."
brooks4444 (02/25/2010, 7:43 AM)

Report Comment

Everyone takes the same test. If you can't pass the test move on and choose another career. This world is not equal like Utopia, it's a competiteve world where the best rise to the top.
BC
mrc1932 (02/25/2010, 7:41 AM)

Report Comment

Yea right, LOWER THE STANDARDS. When is all this equality balony going to end. Its a competetive world out there. The USA is falling behind in math and the sciences in the world. Would you like to be operated on a doctor that earned his degree and training just because of his color or race? NO, I want the smartest person working on me.
BC
mrc1932 (02/25/2010, 7:38 AM)

Report Comment

SCHOOL OF MEDICINE DIVERSITY RESPONSE COALITION MOBILIZES AGAINST "COMPTON COOKOUT,"

E-mail, February 21, 2010

Date: Sun, February 21, 2010 12:13 pm
To: "histgrads-gsa-l@mailman.ucsd.edu" <histgrads-gsa-l@mailman.ucsd.edu>
Priority: Normal
Options: View Full Header | View Printable Version

Dear Student Leaders:

On behalf of SOM Diversity Response Coalition we would formally like to invite you as students, student leaders, future caring physicians, and humanistic people to unite and support our efforts to mobilize a response against the racist "Compton Cookout" party that was put on by a fraternity at UCSD off campus. If you have not heard about the incident, please read about it by clicking on the link. At the end of this email is a description of the party.

http://www.signonsandiego.com/news/2010/feb/17/outrage-expressed-over-party/

The SOM Diversity Response Coalition is a group of medical students that want to express solidarity with the UCSD undergrad community and the San Diego community to promote diversity and equality on campus and beyond. We are outraged that something like this could happen. However, we also feel that this is an incident that is not isolated. As future physicians, we face health disparities that arise from low socioeconomic status that is historically embedded in racism. Not only that, but the school of medicine has failed to increase our diversity partly because minority students want to attend a university where they will feel comfortable and cared about.

We ask that you please:

1. Join us next Tuesday Feb 23rd at NOON as we march in solidarity toward library walk. We will meet in front of OSA at 12:00pm. Please wear a black shirt or wear a black shirt with your write coat on top.
2. If you have time, please make a poster to represent your ideals.
3. Attend the "teach in" Wednesday, February 24th from 12-2pm at the Price Center East Ballroom as a UNIFIED student body!
4. PLEASE PASS THIS EMAIL ALONG TO ANY GRAD OR UnderGRAD STUDENTS THAT MAYBE INTERESTED IN JOINING US

In Solidarity,

Michelle Contreras
UCSD School of Medicine, LMSA Member
SOM Diversity Response Coalition

In Solidarity, We Will Create Change

Address by Mar Velez, BSU Press Conference, February 24, 2010

My name is Mar Velez and I am a third year MEChistA here at UCSD.

Over 40 years ago, as part of a movement to begin diversifying the newly established University of California at San Diego, the Mexican-American Youth Association and the Black Student Council at the time, came together to begin drafting historical/herstorical changes so that the university would begin to serve and become accountable to their two disenfranchised communities. In an efforts to realize a third world college, The Lumumba-Zapata College, they saw the great impact and effect their communities had when they came together in solidarity. Forty years later we are still working together in solidarity and still seeing the same exclusion of our communities at UC San Diego. As part of MEChA and the underrepresented student population on campus I am here to let all of you know that this attack, although targeted toward the culture of the Black population at UCSD, was an attack on all the student of color community on this campus.

This "Compton Cookout" party is a mere window into the kind of exclusion, hostility and marginalization that we as students of color have to endure on a day-to-day basis at UCSD. This kind of day-to-day racism is not just conceded through a party by a few individuals. Rather, this uncomfortable climate for my compañeros and campañeras is produced by the kind of institutional neglect towards the needs of students of color in a higher education setting like UCSD. Placing more importance on its prestige and exclusivity for the wealthy and privileged, UCSD condones an environment that is unsafe and violent to students who come from working class backgrounds, who are first generation college students and that come from under-resourced communities, like

Photo courtesy of Chris Perreira.

myself. I am now a third year, but since my first year I was keenly aware of how this environment made me feel isolated and unsafe. If it were not for the small yet very strong entities on campus like the Cross Cultural Center, the LGBTRC, The Women's Center and one of the most important offices for underrepresented students, OASIS, our community would be even smaller than the 1.3% African Americans, or the 9% of Mexican/Mexican-Americans. And yet these resources are constantly in risk of their funds being cut. These kinds of threats are death sentences to the student of color population at UCSD. And this has been a imminent concern long before this incident. As early as 2006, concerns were brought up by the UCSD Chicano Concilio made up of faculty, staff, and students. Through a series of emails with the Chancellor Marye Ann Fox we expressed our concern about the toxic campus climate being a ticking time bomb for the wellness of underrepresented students. In an email we asked for the Chancellor to create a Task Force on Campus Climate. Here we stated:

"We asked specifically for a task force or advisory committee that could implement a series of action plans in a short amount of time. Our fear is that there is a basic misunderstanding here and that the campus' traditional practice of delaying meaningful action has been reproduced in your response."

Four years later in 2010 we now see the consequences of this university's tradition of delaying implementation of changes for students of color and for overall climate on this campus. Our community efforts and mobilizations today are a clear message that we will not be ignored any longer. This university can no longer run rampant ignoring the needs of students of color and underrepresented students. This kind of neglect and irresponsibility will be exposed and we will make this university accountable to us from here on.

In solidarity, we will create change.

Solidarity through Adversity

Address by Sam Jung, BSU Press Conference, February 24, 2010

Hello. My name is Sam Jung and I am a proud Korean-American that stands in solidarity with my Black brothers and sisters, and I am here to say that we, as a university are in A STATE OF EMERGENCY! For all students and particularly students of color, this is your call to action!

And for those students of color who don't think that these past two weeks of blatant racism and oppression don't have anything to do with you, then I have this to say:

If you have ever been asked, "Can you actually see through your small eyes?"—Because yes, I *can*, this issue effects *you.*

If you have ever been told to "go back to your own country", even though your peoples were here first, this issue affects *you.*

If you have ever been asked "What are you doing here?"—when you have a right to be there, or "Can you really speak English?"—because Yes, I *can* speak English, or if you have ever experienced any type of oppression solely based on the color of your beautiful skin, the beautiful shape of your eyes, or the joyous tone of your voice, then the "Compton Cookout" and the University's lack of REAL ACTION should be a troubling reality for you.

For an injustice against one in our community, is essentially an injustice against all in our community. For we, as students of color regardless of if we identify as Asian-American, a first-Nation person, African-American, a Latino/Latina or a Chicano/Chicana, our collective safety on this campus has been compromised. Hate speech is a weapon that reproduces, justifies, and promotes already existing inequalities which implicates *anyone* and *everyone* who is considered a minority in the country. The enjoyment and consumption of stereotypes in ignorance or in blatant support of perpetuating these inequalities exposes and *marks* individuals and communities as targets of unsanctioned violence—demonstrated throughout history in both the US and the world from racial segregation in Jim Crow society, to colonial genocide in many parts of the world.

We, as students of color are all victims of the pain that comes as a consequence to the use of these stereotypes, which dehumanize us and make us into caricatures of something that we inherently are not; I say this with authority because that is the shared burden and truth of our beautiful skin colors and beautiful facial features in America.

Through this shared experience of humanity we necessarily must find solidarity. Let us, as united students of color, look towards our own history that has so often been written out of the history books that have been used in our schools and acknowledge the strength of racial and ethnic unity that made, but is not limited to, the: United Farm Worker movement, the American Indian movement, the black and yellow movement, the brown within the yellow movement, the Third World Liberation front, and the Black Freedom struggle of the 1950s and '60s.

Ending one of our oppression means ending all oppressions, and although the road has not been easy, to quote Teresa Leal,

> "We have to teach people, this is the way you throw rocks at the sun, despite the fact you know you're not always going to hit it, despite the fact that you are not always going to win. If we were only stimulated by the sure shots, we would never get anywhere; we would be very behind. Change comes only when a few brave hearts dare to throw the first rock."

Even though we, the students of color at UCSD, are not the first ones to have ever fought for social justice, we will continue to be the brave souls that will throw rocks against racism, and hate, to make this university, EXCUSE ME _OUR_ UNIVERSITY, safe for _ALL_ peoples. We must not be disheartened by the bigoted and privileged individuals who seek to terrorize and control us through their perpetuation of systems of oppression, yet seek through optimism, courage, and JOY to undue the damage that has been done at UCSD because

RACISM CAUSES REAL PAIN AND DEMANDS
REAL ACTION. FROM THIS UNIVERSITY.
STUDENTS OF COLOR AND ALLIES UNITE!
POWER TO ALL PEOPLE!
HOLLA BACK YA'LL! HOLLA BACK! HOLLA BACK!

The Problem is Not (Just) the Party.
The Problem is the Party Line.

An open letter to the UC San Diego community
From Professor K. Wayne Yang, Ethnic Studies

Dear us,

First and foremost, we should all commend the Black Student Union and its many allies across the spectrum of student organizations (including fraternities/sororities), for the <u>dignity</u> with which you have faced the recent onslaught of racist provocations. You are turning personal insult into a push for structural changes that are sorely needed at our university. You fight not only for the benefit of African-American students, but for all our common good. You are continuing a tradition of UC San Diego student activism dating at least as far back as 1968. You honor us. I hope our university will honor you back.

That said, I'm not writing to condemn the PIKE party. I'm writing to condemn the university's party line.

University officials have been quick to the condemn the party, and even quicker to point out that it happened "off campus." The party line is one of shock and horror, as if prior to last weekend, this institution was a model of diversity and racial justice. We repeat buzzwords like "mutual respect" and "diversity" and "community" until they are empty of meaning. The party line is to individualize a racist system to a few "racists," and to isolate the event as a freak occurrence at UCSD. This party line says: Let's go after a few fraternity boys, and then go back to business as usual.

WHAT IS BUSINESS AS USUAL?

We have a 1.3% African-American student enrollment, not simply because of poor admissions, but because admitted students don't choose to come to UCSD. Only about 13% of admitted African-American students come to

Troy

Does anyone value the constitution any longer. Yes this may have been in bad taste and yes it has overlooked the emotions and feelings of those being made fun of, but the whole thing is a joke. A bad one, but a joke, and last I checked people have the right of assembly? If people want to get together to mock black history month with a racist display they have that right. The party did not infringe on the rights of others! Though you may think this is in bad taste others may find it a joke. Next week you can through a "douche bag white boy frat" party if you want. That is the beauty of living in the USA, supposedly you have freedom to do what you want so long as you are not effecting other peoples rights.

February 25, 2010, 10:18:11 AM PST – Flag – Like – Reply

Guest

The constitution only applies when it works in favor of "certain" people at "certain" times. Free speech is great
when <x> approves of it. A constitutional law class should be made a prerequisite for all new students

February 26, 2010, 6:12:22 AM PST – Flag – Like – Reply

white girl from the o.c.

while these kids had the constitutional right to have this party, they have the RESPONSIBILITY to show humanity to their fellow man... they are a part of a multi-racial institution. and honestly... the sick part is a bunch of spoiled rich kids who probably got daddy to pay for college at a top party school so they could escape the oppression of their sad middle class lives are making fun of impoverished, underprivileged people who may never have any opportunities that match theirs. it's disgusting and it's silly to defend their behavior. it doesn't even make sense. anyone with half a brain knows they were wrong... they just need to admit and apologize and hopefully learn something from it.

February 26, 2010, 10:14:37 AM PST – Flag – Like – Reply

UCSD (compare to 44% at UCLA). This information comes directly from the "Yield Report"—a 2007 UCSD Final Report from the Advisory Committee on Increasing Yield of Underrepresented Students. The Yield Report actually provided multiple strategies for improving campus climate, and for increasing the number of underrepresented students. These recommendations have by-and-large NOT been implemented despite 2 years of research and 3 years of reading time.

Business as usual means that for the last 30 years our university has refused to repatriate Native American human remains found on the ancient burial ground (on top of which the Chancellor's house now stands). This outright defies federal law and treaty rights. San Diego has the largest number of Native American reservations of any county in the United States, but UCSD has a nearly 0% Native American student body. Why wouldn't Native American students want to come here? It's not just because of some frat parties.

All the administrative condemnations of a woefully misconceived fraternity party will not increase African-American enrollment at UC San Diego. All the email links to the "Principles of Community" will not make UC San Diego more diverse. A Chancellor-sponsored Teach-In, however well intentioned, will not lead to systemic change. Even as a symbolic gesture, it is misdirected—enough so that we should teach against this Teach-In.

WHAT EXACTLY DOES THIS TEACH-IN TEACH?

The Teach-In puts the blame for racism on our students. It exonerates the "teachers" of their role in perpetuating a poor campus climate. If our administration refuses to take responsibility for a toxic campus climate, for our share in the disrespect of African-American, Native American, and other excluded communities, then why would we expect our students to act differently? If our administration deals with collective problems by disavowing individuals, then why would we expect students to act differently? If our administration is silent about its own poor track record in race and community relations, then why would we expect students to act differently?

Furthermore, a two-hour Teach-In trivializes the work of teachers who critically examine race and racism year-round. We teach in History, Ethnic Studies, and Psychology, as well as other programs, departments and colleges, such as Thurgood Marshall's Dimensions of Culture. In these classes, our students and instructors put in intense intellectual and personal work in struggling with our inheritance of racism, sexism, and classism.

But most importantly, teach-ins are strategies for the powerless, not for people in power. The Chancellor has a wide-range of powers and more than a few resources to commit to improving campus climate. The BSU is rightfully pressuring the administration to administrate, not just talk about, solutions for improving our campus climate.

WHAT SHOULD THE ADMINISTRATION DO?

To paraphrase Cornel West, "Young people don't want to hear a sermon, they want to *see* a sermon." It's time to commit to some real structural changes. We can start with the BSU demands. But if a simpler list is needed, I have some suggestions below.

1. **Implement the Yield Report.** This report came out 3 years before last week's frat party. Can the administration take this state of emergency and finally implement the Yield Report recommendations?

2. **Put some teeth into the diversity office.** Currently, the Chief Diversity Officer is a 50% position with no budget, no staff, and no formal power. Upgrade it to a Vice Chancellorship and equip it with a staff and budget. Such offices at UCLA and UC Berkeley are able to provide material support for research, teaching, and student affairs. They can take a preventive approach to racial incidents on campus. (This recommendation can also be found on page 10 of the Yield Report.) But don't stop there. Give this office wide reform powers over all units on the campus, and we will gain at least one institutionalized motor for bridging the gap between the rhetoric and the reality of diversity.

3. **Fund organizations that support underrepresented students.** Right now, student organizations like the SAAC orgs (BSU, MECHA, and others) are doing the work of the administration to recruit, retain, and respect underrepresented students. These student leaders bear a double burden—even as they are assailed by a toxic campus climate, they are also expected to be its antidote. How do we expect to retain our current students if they are mending our university on top of their obligations to schoolwork, jobs, and family? These orgs should be given increased funding for major events such as high school conferences, overnight recruitment events, and graduation ceremonies. (This recommendation is on page 9 of the Yield Report).

4. **Created a <u>committed</u> commission on campus climate.** No, <u>not</u> a group of Chancellor's appointees, but a coalition of organizations with a track record of transforming our university. Start with the SAAC orgs, the Campus Centers, and the interdisciplinary departments and programs.

5. **Repatriate, Research, and Respect.** If diversity is to be more empty word, then it has to become part of the fundamental bus of universities: research, teaching, and service. Fund collaboratories and cluster hires around indigenous scholarship, black and black diaspora studies, and chicano/latino studies. Develop curriculum and coursework relevant to these areas. (These recommendations are on page 10 of the Yield Report). But don't stop there. Repatriate the Native remains, the burial grounds, and the Chancellor's house on it. Let the Kumeyaay decide how they wish to establish a Native peoples' presence on campus. UCSD would lose an unoccupied house, gain a Native cultural hub, and comply with the law. We might also become a truly attractive option for both established and aspiring Native American scholars.

WHAT SHOULD THE FACULTY DO?

As departments, programs, divisions, and as the faculty senate, we should formally endorse the BSU demands and the Yield Report recommendations. We should change our admissions policy from comprehensive to holistic. But don't stop there. Let us create admissions criteria that value local San Diego community knowledge, especially the community intelligence it takes to persevere within structurally disadvantaged schools. We would not only increase campus diversity, but also demonstrate commitment to the local community in these adverse economic times. UC San Diego might yet live up to our namesake.

WHAT CAN STUDENTS DO?

It is a privilege to teach here at UC San Diego, where I am constantly impressed by our students' initiative, compassion, and sense of social justice. Stay up, stay strong, and stay righteous. You're changing this campus.

With respect,

K. Wayne Yang, Assistant Professor of Ethnic Studies
Affiliated Professor of Urban Studies and Planning

The Black Student Union, alongside our staff, faculty, and student allies, would like to make this statement.

The university and our community will not be restored through a two-hour teach-in only accessible to a small part of our campus community, but through the administration's implementation of our demands and the recommendations that have been made to Chancellor Fox since 2006 to improve the environment for underrepresented students on this campus. But most importantly, teach-ins are strategies for the powerless, not for people in power. The chancellor has a wide range of powers, and more than a few resources, to commit to improving campus climate. A teach-in organized by and controlled by the administration reflects the hierarchical approach that the university has taken to address the issues of racism and misogyny on campus and their failure to take the experiences, needs, and demands of the students seriously.

We do not need to focus on the condemnation of individual racist acts but to realize that individual acts of racism, such as the Compton Cookout and the Koala broadcast, are examples of a trickle-down effect, and that racism, classism, sexism, and homophobia that is our campus climate is a direct reflection of the racism and classism that the institution continues to practice. The university does not just need healing; it needs the kind of institutional transformation that can only come by finally listening to those that it has continuously ignored and silenced.

The university and this administration has refused to take action for too long. The UCSD administration is at fault for the fear, discomfort, alienation, and anger being experienced by students on this campus, and the chancellor and vice chancellor must hold themselves accountable. There are institutional problems within this university that need to be changed. The chancellor and vice chancellor have the privilege, power, resources, and authority to make those changes immediately. Change is not produced through bureaucracies of inaction but through the empowerment of students, because this is WHOSE UNIVERSITY?

Crowd:
OUR UNIVERSITY!

Jasmine:
We will not allow this issue to be ignored.

Fnann Keflezighi:
So if you truly care about the campus climate, and healing our community, and making institutional changes on this campus, then I call on you to stand in solidarity with the students unwilling to tolerate the current state of emergency. We want to WALK OUT of this university-sponsored teach-in, because a teach-in is not what is needed right now. Right now, real action is needed. So please join me in OUR teach-in, and follow me to march out of this room!

Crowd:
WHOSE UNIVERSITY?
OUR UNIVERSITY!
WHOSE UNIVERSITY?
OUR UNIVERSITY!
WHOSE UNIVERSITY?
OUR UNIVERSITY!
WHOSE UNIVERSITY?
OUR UNIVERSITY!

Photo courtesy of Erik Jepsen.

PART 2
(RE)ACTION

Photo courtesy of Erik Jepsen.

UCSD
CAMPUS NOTICE
University of California, San Diego

OFFICE OF THE CHANCELLOR

February 4, 2010

ALL ACADEMICS AND STAFF AT UCSD
ALL STUDENTS AT UCSD

SUBJECT: UC San Diego Black History Month, February 2010

I am pleased to announce that UC San Diego will celebrate Black History Month during February with a series of programs and activities focusing on the achievements of African Americans. This year's theme is: UCSD Honors Black History: Recognizing the Future of Black Economic Empowerment.

Activities include talks on the struggle for democracy, human rights and economic empowerment to black history in the United States and worldwide, art exhibits and films exploring the history of African Studies in the United States, black identity, race, and social justice. Events include a luncheon honoring diversity and equality, the 8th Annual Scholarship Brunch, Umalali: The Garifuna Women's Project, jazz and soul music, a mixed Heritage photo exhibit, selected readings from Audre Lorde, a one-person show by award-winning M'Lafi Thompson and an Afro-Caribbean dance and drumming workshop.

All events are free and open to the public, unless otherwise noted.

To learn more about the month long activities, please visit: http://provost.ucsd.edu/blackhistorymonth/

In recognition of this annual event, I am approving two hours of administrative leave with pay for employees to attend a UC San Diego Black History Month activity. Supervisors, upon request, may approve the use of such leave when the absence does not infringe upon the performance of required job duties or patient care.

On behalf of the campus community, I would like to express our sincere appreciation to the members of the UCSD Black History Month Planning Committee for their work on this celebration.

Please join me, the members of the UCSD Black History Month Planning Committee, and our colleagues and guests as we celebrate Black History Month at UC San Diego.

Marye Anne Fox
Chancellor

Photo courtesy of Erik Jepsen.

"COMPTON COOKOUT" PARTY INVITATION

From Facebook, February 15, 2010

RAGEnts Presents: Compton Cook Out

Type:	Party - Holiday Party
Network:	Global
Start Time:	Monday, February 15, 2010 at 1:00pm
End Time:	Tuesday, February 16, 2010 at 12:00am
Location:	regents

Description

February marks a very important month in American society. No, i'm not referring to Valentines day or Presidents day. I'm talking about Black History month. As a time to celebrate and in hopes of showing respect, the Regents community cordially invites you to its very first Compton Cookout.

For guys: I expect all males to be rockin Jersey's, stuntin' up in ya White T (XXXL smallest size acceptable), anything FUBU, Ecko, Rockawear, High/low top Jordans or Dunks, Chains, Jorts, stunner shades, 59 50 hats, Tats, etc.

For girls: For those of you who are unfamiliar with ghetto chicks–Ghetto chicks usually have gold teeth, start fights and drama, and wear cheap clothes - they consider Baby Phat to be high class and expensive couture. They also have short, nappy hair, and usually wear cheap weave, usually in bad colors, such as purple or bright red.
They look and act similar to Shenaynay, and speak very loudly, while rolling their neck, and waving their finger in your face. Ghetto chicks have a very limited vocabulary, and attempt to make up for it, by forming new words, such as "constipulated", or simply cursing persistently, or using other types of vulgarities, and making noises, such as "hmmg!", or smacking their lips, and making other angry noises, grunts, and faces.
The objective is for all you lovely ladies to look, act, and essentially take on these "respectable" qualities throughout the day.

Several of the regents condos will be teaming up to house this monstrosity, so travel house to house and experience the various elements of life in the ghetto.

We will be serving 40's, Kegs of Natty, dat Purple Drank – which consists of sugar, water, and the color purple , chicken, coolade, and of course Watermelon. So come one and come all, make ya self before we break ya self, keep strapped, get yo shine on, and join us for a day party to be remembered– or not.

UCSD Students Respond to "Compton Cookout"

Natasia Kalonji and Sam Huang

Natasia Kalonji so remember when we mobilized people for oscar grant?
can we seriously mobilize against the people who did this shit? i'm talking some SERIOUS e-mail blasting. you down?
February 16 at 12:46am

Sam Huang yay--mobilizing! i'm down.

They have dishonored our African cousins! Your story shall be known amongst my people. For honor! For freeeeedom!
February 16 at 2:19am

OFFICE OF THE CHANCELLOR

OFFICE OF THE VICE CHANCELLOR - STUDENT AFFAIRS

February 16, 2010

ALL ACADEMICS AND STAFF AT UCSD
ALL STUDENTS AT UCSD

SUBJECT: Condemnation of Off-Campus Party and Affirmation of Principles of Community

We were distressed to learn that over the weekend an offensively themed student party, mocking the commemoration of Black History Month, took place off campus. We strongly condemn this event and the blatant disregard of our campus values. Although the party was not a UC San Diego student-organization sponsored event, participants did include UC San Diego students and that causes us great concern.

As stated in our Principles of Community, http://blink.ucsd.edu/HR/policies/POC/principles-of-community.html, we reject acts of discrimination based on race, ethnicity, gender, age, disability, sexual orientation, religion, and political beliefs, and, we will confront and appropriately respond to such acts. We reaffirm our Principles of Community http://blink.ucsd.edu/HR/policies/POC/principles-of-community.html and encourage the campus to join us in our affirmation.

In addition, we invite students, staff and faculty to participate in a teach-in from noon to 2 p.m. on February 24 in the Price Center East Ballroom to explore how such incidents continue to occur today and to discuss the importance of mutual respect and civility on our campus.

Marye Anne Fox
Chancellor

Penny Rue
Vice Chancellor - Student Affairs

There are racially themed parties thrown all the time at every college, every weekend! Our society is full of ghetto people right? Doesn't necessarily mean we are talking about black people every time the word ghetto is brought up. Question, if you ask anyone, how is Compton portrayed in the mass media? Go to youtube and type in Compton and see what comes up. As the looks of it, they were justifying what its like in Compton. I'm not saying it's unfortunate that the description of the invitation matches the appearance of Compton; the individuals associated with the city seems somewhat proud of their appearance and continue to flaunt it with pride. In my opinion, a part of black history was celebrated in this BBQ. If they're going to make such a big deal about it, the should put this much effort into changing the image of Compton so the [right image] of a Compton BBQ could be thrown accepted by society. As far as I see it, great job with the BBQ; it's exactly how Snoop Dogg, WC, Ice Cube, B.E.T, 2pac, and hundreds of other people of influence has described life in this city. If you don't want things to happen like this again, then you should once again take control of black people, especially in Compton since its essentially been done before, and tell them lose their identity so no one emulates them through a party.
February 26, 2010, 12:12:21 PM PST - Flag - Like - Reply

himself2
Actually, when you talk about the word ghetto in the U.S. OF COURSE you're talking about black people – as members of a disadvantaged group their socio-economic status means that they're poor which means that they're living in run-down forgotten areas of the inner city rich white people only notice when they need something to make fun of.

This party is not at all like Snoop Dog, Ice Cube, WC, or 2pac – they are all examples of black people speaking out about their own experience, the problems of poverty and the inner city violence that results from society devaluing and forgetting about a subset of its people. There's a world of difference between speaking up for yourself and having someone else place their ideas about who you are on your back and use these stereotypes to dehumanize you further than society has already.

Outrage Over UCSD Party Mocking Black Culture

Eleanor Yang Su, San Diego Union Tribune
Wednesday, February 17, 2010 at 12:02 a.m.

LA JOLLA - A weekend party that involved University of California San Diego students and mocked Black History Month has drawn the ire of black students and prompted a condemnation sent to all students and faculty by the chancellor.

An invitation to the "Compton Cookout" event urged participants to wear chains, don cheap clothes and speak very loudly, according to wording circulated by outraged students and verified by campus administrators.

As a guide for girls attending the event, the invitation read, "For those of you who are unfamiliar with ghetto chicks—Ghetto chicks usually have gold teeth, start fights and drama, and wear cheap clothes. ..."

Several disgusted students and faculty met with campus administrators last night about the event, which was linked to members of a fraternity.

"These are the people I go to school with and knowing that they're mocking my culture and the history of black people is really offensive," said UCSD sophomore Elize Diop of Los Angeles. "I would like to see the fraternity get reprimanded."

Campus officials say they likely won't discipline any students associated with the event.

"Because it wasn't a UCSD-sanctioned event, or run by a student organization, it doesn't appear that there was a technical violation," said Jeff Gattas, UCSD's executive director of communications and public affairs. "At this point, we don't have a reason to penalize them."

Marye Anne Fox, the campus chancellor, learned about the event yesterday morning, Gattas said, and e-mailed a statement to 29,000 students and 26,000 staff.

"We were distressed to learn that over the weekend an offensively themed student party, mocking the commemoration of Black History Month, took place off campus," her statement read. "We strongly condemn this event and the blatant disregard of our campus values."

She urged students and staff to attend a teach-in on Feb. 24 "to explore how such incidents continue to occur today and to discuss the importance of mutual respect and civility on our campus."

Some faculty members said the party is all the more damaging for the university because of its long struggle in recruiting black students and professors. Blacks make up less than 2 percent of undergraduates.

"I think that the extremely small number of black students and faculty we have and the invisibility of a curriculum focused on the black community and its history makes it easier for this kind of event to take place," said Jorge Mariscal, a literature professor. "There's something about the climate here that drives black students away."

The university publicly identified the party planners only as a group of students.

But an e-mail obtained by *The San Diego Union-Tribune* from Gary Ratcliff, assistant vice chancellor for student life, linked the event to Pi Kappa Alpha fraternity.

"It was not an official Pike event, but the students who posted it on Facebook were members of Pike and other frats," he wrote.

Ratcliff did not return calls.

Members of the fraternity declined to answer questions, saying that their president would be releasing a statement, although none was issued by deadline.

Spencer Washom, a member who graduated in December, said the fraternity is known for having strong athletics, organizing philanthropic events and being diverse.

"I never really found someone who wasn't courteous or respectful of other people," Washom said. "I couldn't see someone doing anything deliberately racist."

An Open Letter from the Campus Community Centers Regarding 2/13 Weekend Events

February 19, 2010

This past weekend, a number of events have occurred that have deeply impacted our community. The inciting incident was the advertising of an off campus party with racist themes. The subsequent events include many responses from numerous quarters of our campus community, including students, faculty, staff, alumni and the greater San Diego community.

Deeply troubling is, while this event clearly targeted historical contributions of African Americans, equally insidious messages were present. The blatant misogyny, glaring class issues, and subtle heterosexism are intertwined throughout the obvious racism. The references to men and women, when juxtaposed, highlight a vast difference in how gender, relationships and class intersect into stereotype, myth and denigration.

This incident underscores the important nature of the work around intersectionality. When one group is targeted, all of our communities are impacted. Incidents such as these, when they happen, can serve to disaffect those from other marginalized communities as well, and pit folks against each other in a hierarchy of oppression.

There were opportunities to stop this event from happening. When individuals expressed concerns about the nature of the party, were they heard? Building community on our campus provides opportunities where these voices can have an impact on decisions that peers make. Critical dialogue can be uncomfortable, but creates a campus climate where all people are valued.

Our communities cannot be bystanders to events such as this. It cannot be "Oh, look what is happening to 'that' group …" We are deeply connected as members of the UC San Diego community, and what affects

Photo courtesy of Cutler Edwards.

one of us affects all of us. It is how we react from our places of privilege that is the true testament of community building.

What we do now, in support and in community with those who have been the most affected, reflects the mission of the Campus Community Centers, which includes the belief that ending one oppression requires ending all oppression.

We invite you to continue the dialogue with us, and to join the teach-in on Wednesday, February 24th from 12-2pm at the Price Center East Ballroom.

IT'S ESCALATING ... KOALA AIRED A SHOW THIS EVENING

Posted to stopracismucsd.wordpress.com, February 19, 2010

HEY FAMILY:

JUST SO YOU KNOW. CAMPUS CLIMATE IS GETTING WORSE, BECAUSE WE ARE NOT BEING HEARD. OUR PAIN CONTINUES TO BE A SOURCE OF MOCKERY AND WE CONTINUE TO BE DISREGARDED BY THE UNIVERSITY AT EVERY LEVEL. STUDENT FUNDED TELEVISION WAS ABUSED TONIGHT IN WHICH THE KOALA USED RACIAL EPITHETS TO TARGET ALL RACIAL GROUPS (THIS IS NOT JUST A "BLACK" THING ANYMORE) OVER LIVE BROADCAST.

ACTIONS AND WORDS THAT CONTINUE TO TARGET PEOPLE OF COLOR IS A CLEAR CONSEQUENCE OF LACK OF A FIRM STANCE ON THE PART OF ADMINISTRATION TO PUNISH RACISTS AND SEXISTS AND TO DEFEND THEIR STUDENTS, THE LARGEST INVESTORS AT UCSD. THE LACK OF TANGIBLE ACTION: WE MEAN E-MAILS ADDRESSED TO THE STUDENT POPULATION, AS EMPTY WORDS; WE MEAN THE CONTINUAL PROTECTION OF FIRST AMENDMENT RIGHTS WHILE OTHERS MUST

STAND BY SILENCED; WE MEAN THE DEPRIORITIZING IN SOCIAL VALUE AND FINANCIAL SUPPORT OF STUDENT-INTIATED AND STUDENT-RUN ACCESS AND RETENTION PROGRAMS, EVEN THOUGH IT IS WELL-KNOWN THAT DURING TIMES OF BUDGET CUTS AND MASSIVE TUITION INCREASES STUDENTS OF COLOR ARE DISPROPORTIONATELY NEGA-TIVELY AFFECTED; WE MEAN THE INCAPABILITY TO HOLD STUDENTS WHO FEEL SAFE AT UCSD TO THE PRINCIPLES OF COMMUNITY AND THE HOSTILE CAMPUS THEY CONTINUALLY CREATE; AND THE REAL INABILITY AND LACK OF MOTIVATION TO ACTUALLY ADDRESS RACISM AT AN INSTITUTIONAL LEVEL. THESE EXAMPLES SIGNAL THE CONDON-MENT OF RACISM AND SEXISM ON OUR CAMPUS, AND CONTINUED INVESTMENT IN WHITE PATRIARCHAL SUPREMACY.

NOW, YOU CAN NO LONGER SAY THAT THIS IS JUST A STUDENT FIGHT. THERE WILL BE NO DIFFERENCE ON OUR CAMPUS UNLESS WE ARE REINFORCED BY ACTUAL INVESTMENT FROM THE UNIVERSITY AT THE INSTITUTIONAL LEVEL TO STOP THIS AND IMPROVE LIFE FOR ALL CURRENT AND FUTURE PEOPLE OF COLOR. THIS FRAT "INCIDENT" CAN NO LONGER BE JUST MADE A LEARNING EXAMPLE, PEOPLE MUST BE HELD ACCOUNTABLE AND PUNISHED FOR THE DECISIONS THEY CONSCIOUSLY AND PURPOSEFULLY MAKE.

IN RESPONSE, WE WILL BE GATHERING ON LIBRARY WALK, AT 8AM AS A SOLIDIFIED COMMUNITY AGAINST RACISM TO DEMAND REAL AC-TIONS BE TAKEN AGAINST THE MULTIPLE "BLACK HISTORY MONTH" EVENTS, THE SOUTH OF THE BORDER PARTY THAT OCCURRED THIS MONTH AND THE COUNTLESS RACIALLY CHARGED EVENTS THAT GO UNNOTICED. PLEASE WEAR BLACK AND JOIN US.

LOVE AND SOLIDARITY,
FNANN AND MABEL

"FYI...I'M ON THE PHONE WITH THE UCSD BSU CHAIR AND HE'S RELAYED TO ME THAT THERE ARE WHITE STUDENTS ON THE UCSD STUDENT RUN TV CALLING THE BLACK STUDENTS "N" WORDS, SAY-ING THEY RECEIVED A PASS AND MOCKING THEM FOR BEING UPSET.

DAVID IS DESCRIBING THEIR FRUSTRATION AND ANGER AND SAYS THAT HE AND THE OTHER STUDENTS DO NOT FEEL SAFE AND DO NOT TO WANT TO BE ON CAMPUS. STUDENTS ARE CRYING AND DEEPLY UPSET OVER THIS SITUATION AND HAVE CALLED UCPD. I ALSO SPOKE WITH DIANE GRIFFITHS, THE SECRETARY AND LEFT A MESSAGE FOR JUDY SAKAKI TO RESPOND. WE CALLED THE CHIEF OF STAFF FOR MARY ANNE FOXX AND LEFT HER MY NUMBER TO CALL BACK IMMEDIATELY. WE'VE NOT BEEN ABLE TO GET A HOLD OF ANYONE ON THE CAMPUS, EXCEPT UCPD, BUT THEY WILL CERTAINLY HEAR ABOUT IF FIRST THING IN THE MORNING. THIS IS NOT GOOD."

Subject: Racism Response press conference tomorrow--please attend
From: ccedward@ucsd.edu
Date: Tue, February 23, 2010 2:15 pm
To: "histgrads-gsa-l@mailman.ucsd.edu" <histgrads-gsa-l@mailman.ucsd.edu>
Priority: Normal
Options: View Full Header | View Printable Version

Before the "diversity teach-in" at Price Center tomorrow at noon, there
will be a press conference on library walk beginning at 10 am. The BSU
has requested that sympathetic parties come out to show support and make a
visible presence. I hope to see you there

Download this as a file

Rallying the Student Protesters Occupying the UCSD Chancellor's Complex

Professor Daniel Widener, History, February 26, 2010

How's everybody feeling!? (cheering and applause)

So, a couple of quick things: First of all, congratulate yourselves: You are occupying the heart of the University of California at San Diego!

I don't know how many of you are at your first demonstration today and how many of you were able to come out on Wednesday, but on Wednesday we said "No more business as usual." We said "the old UCSD is finished, and the new UCSD is about to begin." WELCOME TO DAY THREE OF THE NEW UCSD!

As you know, time is running out for the administration but they have a few minutes left, and we wanted to fill a few of those minutes with a couple of things that I think are an important part of summarizing and understanding our day ... .

A few folks want to have a few words about especially about how to sustain and connect this energy. I just want to update folks:

It seems there was a demonstration today at Berkeley.

It seems there was a demonstration today at UCLA.

I don't know how many of you know this, but the people who run this university wake up every morning wanting to be like Berkeley and they want to be like UCLA.

But today the people at Berkeley and at UCLA, they woke up, and they decided they wanted to be like us!

Minorities should not be looking to the school to "boost their numbers". They should be doing that themselves by: getting better grades in high school; taking college preparatory classes, Advanced Placement or Honors classes, scoring higher on the SAT and ACT; even actually applying to the University. The party was in poor taste but it was mocking a particular sub sect of inner city life that minorities should be trying to rid themselves of rather than yelling at people who point out their flaws. White people make fun of "rednecks", "crackers", "hillbillies" and "white trash". And so do black people. But we don't hold press conferences and rallies over insults directed at the morons of our race so grow some thicker skin and don't behave in a way that would confuse people about your personal character.
WorkingCitizen (02/25/2010, 7:21 AM)

Report Comment

Party Foul Offended Students and Administration Respond to Racially Themed Frat Cookout

Angela Chen, The Guardian, February 18, 2010

An event invitation to a ghetto-themed party titled "Compton Cookout" has incited outrage among black students and supporters on campus, who held a Campus Black Forum on Tuesday night to discuss the issue. The forum was hosted by the Students for Affirmative Action Committee, a coalition of diversity-minded campus groups including the Black Student Union.

The party was held Monday—"in hopes of showing respect" to Black History Month—by a group of individuals affiliated with a number of fraternities; particularly, Pi Kappa Alpha. The event received notoriety when the Facebook event description was published in a note by Revelle College sophomore Elize Diop. The party called for males to wear "XXXL" T-shirts and "stunner shades," and for females to dress like "ghetto chicks" in cheap clothing. Approximately 275 students RSVPed as "attending."

The matter was brought to the attention of Chancellor Marye Anne Fox and Vice Chancellor of Student Affairs Penny Rue Monday night by e-mails from concerned students. Fox and Rue sent out a mass e-mail early Tuesday morning condemning the party as "a blatant disregard of our campus values."

"As soon as we realized it was not a hoax, we worked to respond as quickly as possible," Rue said.

Students attending Tuesday's forum said they were not directly targeting the fraternity, but were more concerned about the lack of awareness about diversity on campus. Currently, less than 2 percent—or 200 of the campus' 22,000 undergraduate students—is registered as black.

According to Warren College junior Cierra McCoy, the party is only a symptom of the lack of campus diversity. She said that black students not only have low acceptance and yield rates, but also low retention rates, as many of them eventually want to transfer due to racism at the university.

"There's all this talk about improving student life," McCoy said at the forum. "Well, this is my student life. I don't give a damn if the National Guard has to walk me to my bio class, I will make them do it, and I will not transfer, and I will graduate."

Other forum attendees, such as A.S. Campuswide Senator Bryant Pena, called for the expulsion of the individuals involved in planning the party.

However, Rue said that it is unlikely that the university will take direct action against these students.

"I do not believe there will be punishment as this still falls under the protection of free speech," she said.

She said the university would focus on diversity campaigns instead.

"I believe the best way to respond to this type of speech is more speech, since it's our collective voices that show the resilience of the San Diego community," she said.

Both Director of Student Life Emily Feinstein—who is also the Inter-Fraternity Council adviser—and Director of Student Involvement Emily Marx said the event was neither funded nor sponsored by a fraternity.

"The only fraternity link this has is that some of the organizers were Greek-affiliated," IFC president Robby Naoufal said. "We can't control the conduct of our members every moment of the day. They do act on their own."

Marx agreed.

"We found out that it is individuals who did this—that it was multiple members of the same [apartment complex], and not fraternity-sponsored," she said.

However, Feinstein said the university is meeting with the individuals involved—whose named have not been released—and that various Greek organizations will work with local and national chapters to educate them about the incident.

"I will do everything in my power to rehabilitate not just the Greeks, but [to] try to empower the entire community," she said.

Campuswide Senator Tobias Haglund, who is also a member of the IFC, denied allegations,—including Diop's—accusing PIKE of being a "white frat".

"That is absolutely false," he said. "We pride ourselves on our diversity. Whoever made the comment was rightly upset and emotional, but PIKE is not a white frat."

PIKE issued an official statement today denying association with the Compton Cookout and condemning the party.

Students also used Tuesday's forum as an opportunity to speak out against controversial humor newspaper the Koala. They cited the most recent issue—which ridiculed the Jan. 12 earthquake that devastated Haiti—as well as past issues that have repeatedly used the word "nigger."

According to Assistant Vice Chancellor of Student Life Gary Ratcliff, the cookout and Koala content are both representative of prejudice on campus.

"The Koala is the journalistic equivalent to an arsonist," he said. ""It gets pleasure from the terror of others."

Ratcliff added that he would support withdrawing funding from the publication, though a recent A.S. proposal to alter media guidelines was unsuccessful.

"For 10 years I've seen cycles of Koalas injure students," he said. "I've worked with leaders to set up meetings about this issue. A courageous group went to the A.S. [Council] to talk about it, but [the council] got cold feet."

A.S. Associate Vice President of Diversity Affairs Jasmine Phillips said the university constantly marginalizes minorities; for instance, by asking the BSU to pay for its own yield program, which is designed to encourage minority students to graduate.

"The administration expects our organization to [shell out] for the yield [program] when it's their problem that they should be working on it themselves," she said. "We can't just keep planning—something needs to happen."

In response to the recent upset, administrators are launching a diversity campaign called "Not in Our Community," and will be holding a teach-in on Feb. 24 from 12 p.m. to 2 p.m. in the Price Center East Ballroom.

---

 gordonwagner 02/27/2010 10:49 AM in reply to Juneone

It's a hilarious concept, and it's NOT POLITICALLY CORRECT!!!! Black culture is often unintentionally hilarious to white people (and everyone else). Grape soda and Cheetos? The whole "ebonics" thing? Street gang membership? Yes, I can see where this would be a target-rich environment for parody. It's FUNNY. Because it's NOT politically correct! Being politically correct is what ought to be examined here, really. Thin-skinned, overly sensitive students with hurt feelings? Next story, plz.

Flag

 Juneone 02/27/2010 12:36 PM in reply to gordonwagner

Next story was the noose.

I am not sure what "politically correct" means. I realize it is a buzz word for some, but would you care to explain what you mean by that? You don't need to do it now, just maybe the next time you use it.

Flag

Photo courtesy of Erik Jepsen.

BSU Chairpersons Address the Crowd at Rally in Response to Noose Hung in Geisel Library

Fnann Keflegizhi and David Ritcherson, February 26, 2010

DAVID: ... THIS IS AN ISSUE OF SAFETY RIGHT NOW. THERE ARE UNDER-COVER COPS, THERE ARE SPIES AMONG THE CROWD, SO PLEASE BE AWARE OF THAT. ANY CONVERSATIONS YOU'RE HAVING ABOUT ANY PLANS YOU WANT TO DO, ANY FURTHER STEPS OF ACTION, WHISPER THOSE, OR WAIT UNTIL WE LEAVE. THIS IS SERIOUS ... THERE ARE PEOPLE OUT HERE WE CAN'T TRUST.

IT IS NICE THAT THE UNIVERSITY HAS CAUGHT THIS PERSON [WHO HUNG THE NOOSE]—OR IS IN CONTACT WITH THE PERSON WHO DID THIS. BUT THAT'S NOT THE ISSUE RIGHT NOW—THE ISSUE IS THE STEPS THAT NEED TO BE TAKEN BY THE ADMINISTRATION THAT HAVEN'T BEEN TAKEN. AS OF RIGHT NOW, THE UNIVERSITY HAS UNTIL 5PM TODAY TO PRODUCE THE PROJECT GRID OF OUR DEMANDS. WE ARE WAITING ON THAT.

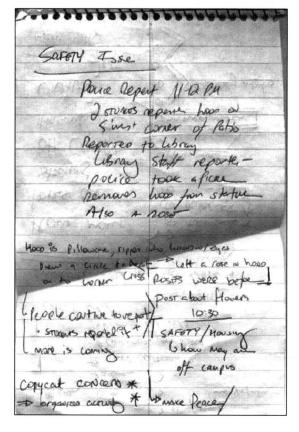

AS WELL AS THAT, THEY ARE SETTING UP A MEETING WITH THE ACADEMIC SENATE WHICH I GUESS PRETTY MUCH RUNS EVERYTHING ON THIS CAMPUS. THOSE ARE THE IMPORTANT PEOPLE—THOSE ARE THE PEOPLE WE NEED TO TALK TO. AS OF NOW, WE DON'T WANT TO ABUSE THE POWER AND THE SPACE THAT WE HAVE. THERE HAS BEEN A SUGGESTION TO DO A MARCH, TO DO MORE RALLIES, BUT THAT'S NOT THE BEST OPTION RIGHT NOW—WE'RE GOING TO STAY OUT HERE AS LONG AS WE CAN, BUT WE ARE ALSO GOING TO TRY TO COOPERATE WITH THE ADMINISTRATION AS MUCH AS POSSIBLE.

SO KEEP THAT IN MIND—WE DO HAVE THINGS ON THE WAY. WE ARE WINNING. AMONGST ALL THIS CHAOS, WE ARE WINNING, WE ARE GETTING SHORT-TERM WINS.

SO KEEP THAT IN MIND. THE UNIVERSITY HAS UNTIL 5PM. WE ARE GOING TO HOLD THEM ACCOUNTABLE. THEY NEED TO BE SETTING UP THIS ACADEMIC SENATE MEETING—RIGHT CHANCELLOR FOX? OH, SHE ALREADY LEFT … . [LAUGHTER FROM THE CROWD]

FNANN: SO WE JUST WANT TO REITERATE—IF THE UNIVERSITY DOES NOT TAKE REAL ACTION, WE WILL BE FORCED TO TAKE REAL ACTION. AND THEY SHOULD PREPARE THEMSELVES FOR THAT. [WILD APPLAUSE]

UCSD
CAMPUS NOTICE
University of California, San Diego

ASSOCIATED STUDENTS

February 25, 2010

ALL ACADEMICS AND STAFF AT UCSD
ALL STUDENTS AT UCSD

SUBJECT: Student Run Television (SRTV)

On Thursday night, a deeply offensive and hurtful program was aired on Student Run Television (SRTV), a service of the Associated Students. The content of this program does not represent the views of the Associated Students, and was aired by KoalaTV, the television show put on by the student organization The Koala. We condemn the actions of The Koala, its program and its content.

The Koala was not properly authorized to display content on SRTV. We are in the process of determining how the program was aired. In the meantime, as authorized by the ASUCSD Standing Rules, and in conjunction with our Associate Vice President of Student Services, I turned off the station to allow for a review of its Charter. We will only open it again when we can be sure that such hateful content can never be aired again on our student funded TV station.

Alongside this initiative, I have frozen all student media organization funding. The Koala has long since been a controversial publication at UC San Diego and is primarily funded by our student fees. I do not believe we should continue funding this organization with our fees.

We must develop effective policies to ensure that our fees do not go to the support the hateful speech that targets members of our community. I ask that those media organizations that did nothing wrong and are unfairly affected to be patient until we can resolve this situation and develop new funding bylaws for our Association.

To this end, I have charged a campus-wide committee to review the funding of student media. This committee is open to every member of the UC San Diego community - faculty, staff, students, and whoever else feels strongly about this issue. The committee shall meet on Thursday, at 8:00PM, in the 4th floor Price Center Forum. Feel free to email me at aspresident@ucsd.edu if you have any questions.

The Associated Students stands in solidarity with those affected by Thursday night's program, and we remain committed to being the voice for all UC San Diego students.

Utsav Gupta
Associated Students President

Please wear BLACK in solidarity. Rumors afoot of counterdemonstrations. Come out in strength.

Download this as a file

UC Davis Investigates Vandalism Cases as Hate Crimes

Cathy Locke, Sacramento Bee, *February 27, 2010*

University of California, Davis, officials say two recent cases of vandalism on the campus are being investigated hate crimes.

A swastika, carved into a Jewish student's door in the Tercero residence hall, was discovered Feb. 19, said Lt. Matt Carmichael of the UC Davis Police Department.

"It came as a total shock to the student," he said. "She felt they all got along pretty well (in the dormitory)."

Carmichael said the department also is investigating as a hate crime a vandalism incident discovered about 12:30 p.m. today. Graffiti was found on a campus building that houses the Lesbian, Gay, Bisexual, Transgender Resource Center. The graffiti, he said, was clearly intended to be offensive to those the center serves.

In a letter sent Friday to campus faculty and staff, UC Davis Chancellor Linda Katehi cited the swastika incident as one of a series of acts in recent weeks on UC campuses that she described as "reprehensible, inexcusable and an affront to our own campus's Principles of Community."

A week earlier, members of Greek fraternities at UC San Diego allegedly organized an event called the "Compton Cookout." Invitations to the event, Katehi said, encouraged participants to mock Black History Month by promoting negative and offensive racial and gender stereotypes.

Earlier in the month, a group of students attempted to disrupt the Israeli ambassador to the United States during a speech at UC Irvine.

In addition, a noose was found Thursday night hanging from a light fixture in the Geisel Library on the UC San Diego campus. Campus officials said a student came forward Friday morning and claimed she and two others were responsible.

The incidents were condemned in a written statement issued Friday by UC President Mark G. Yudof, chancellors of the 10 UC campuses, and the chairman and vice chairman of the universitywide Academic Senate.

"I'm deeply frightened by the way all this is snowballing on our campuses," Dan Simmons, a UC Davis law professor and vice chairman of the systemwide Academic Senate said Saturday.

Simmons said he thinks people are anxious because of the poor economy, and the university, with layoffs, furloughs and fee hikes, has become the focal point for many of those anxieties.

"People are acting out out of frustration. They see this as an opportunity to strike out," he said. "But none of this does any of us any good. It certainly doesn't accomplish anybody's goals."

Guest
That's what this is all about.. the blacks have and always will want more money. Its about them. Cause they're special. And the rest of us can go to hell 'cause if we object, we're bad people and racist.
February 24, 2010, 1:48:13 AM PST - Flag - Like - Reply

Guest
they're at the front of the bus and now they want VIP treatment
February 24, 2010, 1:52:20 AM PST - Flag - Like - Reply

Guest
they're getting worse than jews
February 24, 2010, 4:04:15 AM PST - Flag - Like - Reply

Photo courtesy of Erik Jepsen.

Dear World,
We're sorry and embarrassed.
Sincerely, most of UCSD.

Ashley Bagnall Davis, Sunday, February 21, 2010 at 7:46pm

I've realized that my pride in UCSD comes singlehandedly from my experiences in the lit and poli sci department, specifically, how much I learned about the history of cultural, ethnic and economic oppression in this country and abroad. The most obvious and relevant example that comes to mind is the history of blackface minstrelsy and how, even as abolition was underway, white people got on stage in blackface makeup and exaggerated and exploited every negative black stereotype they could ... the point of this "entertainment" was to support and perpetuate slavery by showing "comical" images of blacks as shiftless, inferior, lazy, and less than human. Back then people couldn't distinguish propaganda from fact, and it influenced them at the ballot box. So why assume that we are any more capable today?

Obviously we haven't learned anything from our history, or at least the Pi Kappa Alpha fraternity at UCSD hasn't. (But I hope this embarrassment at least gets the ball rolling for them.) Frankly, I don't assume frat boys are intelligent enough to tie their own shoes until they prove me otherwise, much less stop and think about the stupid, insulting, and disrespectful consequences of their thoughtless actions.

I do believe that this massive insult was more a result of ignorance than deliberate racism, but therein lies the problem. Why is ignorance ok, as long as the ignorant person in question doesn't consciously engage in active acts of racism such as physical violence, racial epithets, etc. Why is everyone so damn complacent about the fact that we have a black president? And am I really supposed to believe that in the entire course of planning this "Compton cook-out," not ONE PERSON had enough brains and balls to say "wait a minute, this is not cool and here's why ..."

Here's what I'm getting at. A hundred years ago, someone who was "racist" was not only upfront about it, but aggressive. They toasted whisky glasses to the open despisal of [insert epithet here]. Today's "racist" could very well be someone with an exceptionalist point of view who voted for Obama. Nobody wants to confront ways in which their patterns of thinking are wrong, be it in their spending habits or their racial assumptions. And so nobody will avow themselves as racist. It's the scarlet letter of today's world even though it's still alive ALL OVER THE PLACE. They will excuse themselves because they "have black friends" and then turn around and throw a Compton cook-out.

So back to my original point. I love UCSD. I miss it. (Not too much.) I'm very proud to say I went there and I took classes there that moved me and changed my life. So, original point: This sucks, and it's embarrassing to me as an alumni. Or alumna. Whichever. It is a smack in the face to everything that I hold dear about my school.

PS—as punishment I say we send these silly frat boys to a real bbq in Compton to be dealt with appropriately by the people who were most directly being mocked. Who's with me!!

---

 plomaman 02/28/2010 11:06 PM

Everyone experiences some form of discrimination on a daily basis. Its part of life...living! People discriminate against each other all day long based on clothing, employment status, weight, ethnicity, the color of their hair, sexual orientation, habits, where they live, marital status, what kind of car they drive, how they talk, walk....well, you get the idea! We ALL learn how to deal with it and roll with the punches.

These protesters seem to think and act as if they are the only ones who experience discrimination for crying out loud....theyre actually demanding that they be sheltered from life and everyone has to stop bothering them. I'd be willing to bet that for most of those holding the race cards, ANY competition or discrimination they experience gets filed as an act of racism in their egotistical little brains. Well, its time for them to stop crying ....or mommy and daddy might pull their next allowance check! Enough is enough. We all get it.

YOU'RE QUESTIONING *MY* LEGITIMACY ON THIS CAMPUS? LET ME TAKE YOU TO *MY* THEORETICAL LEVEL

Desiree Prevo and Jaicele Wallace. Friday morning rally in response to noose hanging, March 26, 2010.

Desiree: I am really hurt and sad by what's happening on this campus right now. I don't think it's fair that we have to suffer on so many levels. How many of us have missed classes? How many of us have gone to class but couldn't focus? How many of us had to take midterms? It's not right that we are held responsible like everything is ok, because we can't. We don't have that privilege!

Jaicele: I've been trying to articulate my thoughts inside my head, so I could try to pump up the crowd and everything. And then, as I started thinking about everything, my mind just got mentally exhausted. And my body is physically exhausted, and my emotions are exhausted. And I think I'm tired of everything on this campus.

I'm tired of having to prove my legitimacy on this campus.

When people ask me, why am I *here*? **I'm** here for the same reason that *you're* here:

I got my SAT scores.
I did my essays.
I got my letters of rec.
I'm here for the exact same reasons that you are.
I got in just like you did.
So don't question my legitimacy on this campus.
I got in because I'm intelligent, I'm tenacious, and I'm resilient.

And *you're* questioning **my** legitimacy on this campus? It makes me question *your* legitimacy on this campus."

Desiree: …this meeting* on Wednesday was interesting because the media has somehow spun—or some members of a certain organization on this campus have spun—this overall systemic, institutionalized racism as an issue of free speech.

I just want to speak about free speech. I agree that we do need free speech, and that it's important.

But some people are taking it to a theoretical argument … but if you want to take it to a theoretical level, let me take you to MY theoretical level. Let me explain to you:

The Bill of Rights, from which free speech came, was NEVER meant to include my people, OUR people. So how do you expect

---

*   the UCSD Administration's teach-in.

me to respect your free speech, when I wasn't even meant to HAVE free speech? …

My second point: March 4th—next week, national day of education … some students are working really hard on that. So don't let that get lost, it all relates, it all correlates. So definitely come out to that, research on that. Thank you, in love and solidarity.

---

are those students aware that they simply appear to be racial whiners?
No one, outside of similarly aggrieved "victim" class racists, can empathize.
If more of "your people" aren't in a given institution perhaps "your people's" culture need a "sit-on".
check yourself before you wreck yourself people….
bellinghammond (02/25/2010, 11:19 AM)

Report Comment

EXCERPTS FROM LETTERS WRITTEN BY MY HIGH SCHOOL STUDENTS

Josen Gayle Diaz

Excerpts from Letters written by My High School Students
Saturday, February 27, 2010 at 2:15pm

Not sure of what other direction to go besides in solidarity with the student organizers at UCSD, I ran this afternoon's high school writing workshop around the school-to-prison pipeline and the ways my high school students are implicated in the hate acts perpetuated by this campus. Their freewriting exercise was to write a letter to the BSU. Below are a few excerpts that I want to share: their sophisticated expression of their thoughts and feelings upon learning about the events of the past few weeks are reminders of real pain, real action.

(Love to my homegirl J. Sapigao for the inspiration.)

"The lack of action by the school is even more frustrating. To not do anything about this is like saying that racism is no big deal. BULLOCKS! This is insane! What is this, the 20th century? The racism on this campus says a lot. It says that one of the most prestigious schools in the country thinks that racism is acceptable. It reflects our society, saying that it is okay to mock certain ethnic groups."

"The library already had a first threat, and I am wondering ... how much longer are you guys going to wait in order to take full responsibility against these comments? Is the school going to wait until a tragedy happens in order to listen to their students? Something bad has to occur in campus for the students to be heard? Why not take full actions about this NOW?"

"We the students of Upward Bound give you support of voice and mind. May your power of speech send not only a voice to the people but also in the history of righteous activists."

"I am not African–American, I am Mexican–American and as a different race I can not empathize your anger but I'm for sure furious."

"I feel that UCSD is a great school and it would be great if I could attend this campus. But after what I learned what happened, I'm not quite sure if I want to apply to this school. I feel that way because since I'm a minority I feel threatened by the racist event that the students made."

"I am an African American student and I am aware of the struggles that being a person of color comes with and that we face everyday. Now knowing what happened with the event 'Compton Cookout,' I feel the pain that you all went through. Though this event was wrong, something like this was necessary to bring together all people of color in order to bring awareness to racism and discrimination."

It's college!! Students since the beginning of time have done and said many things that will outrage some. It will never change, it just goes with the territory and the age group of those involved. I say, to those offended, do a flip-side party or something similar. Have an Uptight White Person BBQ - serve mayonaise sandwiches and iced-tea, I don't know. Making this such an overblown and unwarrented political mess is just shining the wrong kind of light on yourselves. Do your work, don't look to everyone else to hand you a career because of your color and get over yourselves.
gclaet (02/25/2010, 9:32 AM)

Report Comment

It is sad that most people here ignore the fact that low minority enrollment today is a sign of systemic racism- persisting from segregation and blatant racism of the past. The 1960s were not too long ago. Educational outreach and programs are indeed owed to minority children who may not have the resources to aspire to a college education on their own and may be the first in their families that can even hope to have a college education due in large part to the ignorance and close minded actions of those in the majority
cmjones0309 (02/25/2010, 9:30 AM)

Report Comment

Race relations within this country will not improve if the minorities use their race, sex or sexual preference as an excuse for not succeeding. Anytime race, sex or sexual preference is used to advance an agenda, it will ultimately result in resentment on the part of the majority. Race, sex or sexual preference should not become an automatic entitlement. Achievement, hard work, perseverance and ability should be the requirements to succeed. Until universities get over their Politically Correct social policies there will always be bad feelings between the minorities and majorities.

Nothing is equal until it is applies equally.
chatmandu (02/25/2010, 9:22 AM)

Report Comment

FORWARD

DEMOCRACY AND LIBERATION

*a revolutionary, multi-issue organizatio
justice through education, student and \
protest, and the development of libe
democratic theory and p*

"A Note to the Privileged at UCSD"

Archibald P. Regenton IV, Forward: Democracy and Liberation
(forwarducsd.org)

This J. Jones thing is crap. (No, I won't use that word, thanks.) He
found a way to attach his name to the so-called Compton cookout
after the fact, even claiming it was his DVD release party, because
he's a no-name hack who cares about nothing but his 15 minutes and
his paycheck. It is very clear from the original invitation that the party
had NOTHING to do with a DVD release from some two-bit sellout.

But, despite the fact that it's obviously total bullshit, people who can't
step outside of their privilege and acknowledge something called
"systemic racism" vs. "individual racism" are afraid of looking behind
the curtain so they grab onto the bullshit desperately. "See? A real
live Compton guy did it! It's not racist! I don't know what all the fuss
is about!" Where were these people when Compton High students
and teachers bared their souls in the price center ampitheater on
Wednesday?

It's frustrating to talk to a lot of my fellow white people because
we're always convincing ourselves that we and the people and groups
we associate with are Not Racist, Not Sexist, Not Homophobic,
etc. Throughout my life, I've noticed how a conversation between
white people can quickly turn into a pat on the back all around for
everyone's commitment to Not Being A Racist (or Sexist or now
Homophobe). As if racism (etc.) were some individual lifestyle choice
instead of a social force affecting billions of people in different places
all at once. Then, with this load of nonsense as a foundation, we
make our detached moral/ethical/political judgments on the matter at

Photo courtesy of Erik Jepsen.

hand. "Hmm, well, my gay friends love this place, and nobody ever discriminates against them! UCSD is just splendid! I can't be bothered to go see what the black students are saying, they must not know that UCSD is Not-Racist/Sexist/Homophobic."

But if you actually spend time at the LGBT center and go to some of the student-run workshops and presentations and go to student meetings (the interesting ones), you'll hear people in pain talking about the hurt that people put on them physically, mentally and emotionally. Every once in a while you'll see a story posted on the wall written by some anonymous student who is right there in the space with you, and as you read the beat-by-beat details of how a guy on campus tried to rape her straight, your stomach will turn. You'll see another story from a transgender student who is phobic of turning in financial aid applications because he'll have to put down his name and whether he puts down his real name or the name he was born with he'll have to do a mountain of explaining through all the red tape. Some people fear having the cops called on them in any public bathroom because no matter which one they choose somebody in there will freak out and make him or her or whoever out to be a monster when xhe is just trying to use the bathroom for once without risking arrest. (That particular battle is being won thanks to student and staff activism at UCSD. It's so fashionable to pooh-pooh student activism nowadays, isn't it? People forget that resources like the Women's Center, the Cross-Cultural Center and the LGBT center were won because students went on hunger strikes and students broke all the windows in the Chancellor's complex.)

Real homophobia (and biphobia, transphobia, etc.) is not something that you just assume isn't a problem because a gay friend tells you life is great and maybe leaves out the not-so-great stuff. "Ask my gay friends—UCSD is great to minorities!" No, real homophobia and other oppressions, like racism, and sexism, and ablism, are everywhere; they are in the air we breathe, in the words we use it for, in our minds at all times, even if we're not thinking about them. They are the foundation of the culture we share and that culture is based on exploiting certain groups of people for the benefit of others. From time to time, the culture crosses the line, and one of those groups rises up and says, "We have tolerated your lies, your human and civil rights abuses, your fire traps, your ropes, your shit jobs, your immiseration of our people, your imperial wars, and your decadent greed, and now you mock us for eking out our own position in the society that belongs to us as well as you? Enough is enough!" This is what we are witnessing at UCSD. Every time someone says, "Well, I know there's no racism problem here, so those protesters are just going overboard", education cries a death wail.

We at UCSD are privileged to have a massive library dedicated to social sciences, history and the humanities. It's called SSH. Go there sometime, and read about something called "systemic racism" and something called "intersectionality". While you're at it, you can take courses in Ethnic Studies and Critical Gender Studies—they're offered here for the explicit purpose of teaching people how to apply critical thinking to intersectionality, and their presence was won through student activism. It is a rare victory in public higher education, where the really cool stuff usually turns out to be subsidized by taxpayer dollars and "education fees" and make profit for some company (making one lucky professor rich while her grad students make minimum wage doing the work). Anyway, I digress: go to SSH library at Geisel, take Ethnic Studies and Critical Gender Studies classes, go to student presentations at the Cross-Cultural Center, the LGBT center, and the Women's Center...basically, try to read like the educated person we all claim to be, and try listening sometimes instead of just talking about all the stuff you know about racism, etc. We'll all be better off for it.

If you're interested in educating yourself on the true nature of discrimination, you'll find that you will also learn the tools for taking apart these criticisms of society themselves. You'll be better able to form your argument, and you'll finally learn how to shed your acculturated assumptions to see things at the root. It's like un-washing your own brain. Try it sometime. You might like it.

Archibald

P. S.—The inevitable complaints from white people are in. The first time some real shit about what white people **do** gets pointed out, somebody's there saying "You're being racist against white people!" (Yet we mock people from other groups for shit they don't even do, and then get surprised that they see it as racist.)

Anyway, I'm a white person and I do plenty of stuff that could probably be described as racist, sexist or homophobic, so don't go thinking I'm out to indict white people on social crimes. No, I'm just trying to advocate for some education, something we have available here at UCSD, and white people need to take advantage of. I make the effort, and I learn the effects of my actions, and I learn how to **teach myself** to make my actions line up a little better with my ideals sometimes. We're all human, we all do things that don't line up perfectly with the things we believe in sometimes—so you don't have to approach these things like you're mortified of getting called a Racist (or a Sexist or a Homophobe). Nobody is trying to out you as a Racist, we're just trying to get you to understand systemic racism and how we all contribute to it, and what we can and should do about it. Don't take it personally—it belongs to everyone.

Photo courtesy of Jessica Cordova.

PART 3
CONSTELLATIONS OF STRUGGLE

Photo courtesy of James Evans.

BSU CHAIRPERSONS, DAVID RITCHERSON AND FNANN KEFLEGIZHI, BSU PRESS CONFERENCE

February 24, 2010

FNANN: Alright, so today we're here together to call for real action on behalf of this university. And I really want to thank everyone for coming out here today, especially for those who have driven down from Los Angeles and other campuses to stand in solidarity with us. Um, well we're gonna go ahead and start today. ... I'd like to introduce David Ritcherson, who is the Black Student Union chair, who's a huge mentor of mine. I feel like the leader I've become has been very much through the guidance he's given me, and how he's empowered me to have a voice on this campus. So ya'll wanna help me in welcoming David?

DAVID: THE BLACK represents the struggle of my people. THE BLACK represents the silent voices of my people. THE BLACK represents the hyper-visibility of my people. THE BLACK represents the *in*visibility of my people. THE BLACK represents the strength of my people.

It is with immediate concern and urgency that a state of emergency must be declared in order to address the hostile and toxic environment being faced by various communities of color at the University of California, San Diego. We are dealing with a destructive campus, in which our safety—in addition to our emotional, physical, and mental wellbeing—are constantly threatened ... .

... [The administration] has constructed a meaning of diversity, along with diversity efforts, that does NOT directly confront the institutionalized racism, classism, sexism, and homophobia faced by historically underrepresented and underserved people of color.

WE affirm diversity is a representation of historically underrepresented racial groups, underprivileged persons of low socioeconomic backgrounds, and women. We assert this definition to be the diversity the university needs to put at the forefront when considering efforts to increase underrepresented and marginalized people of color on this campus. Diversity is not recruiting student from certain regions of the United States; this is a mass effort to privatize the University of California.

The University of California system is not representative of communities of color, low-income communities, and other historically underrepresented and marginalized communities. The detrimental effect of the campus climate that we now witness is only a continuum of institutional, systematic racial inequalities and intolerance that the administration has been well aware of throughout documentations of the 2007 Year Report as well as the Black Student Union's Do UC Us? Campaign. Students in general feel isolated, unsupported, which contributes to the continuous cycle that prevents underrepresented communities from entering this very university. For students of color, queer-identified students, and students from low socioeconomic backgrounds, this has been a continuated struggle to validate our own presence and existence at this university, both socially and academically.

Photo courtesy of Erik Jepsen.

We stand in solidarity and in struggle with all marginalized groups, underrepresented communities at the UCSD campus, which include but not are limited by Native American and indigenous brothers and sisters fighting for the repatriation of their ancestral remains found on the UCSD campus. We understand the subsequent effects for access, yield, retention of indigenous persons who do not feel welcomed and embraced by a campus that continuously disrespects the spirituality and unique culture of the native nations. In addition, we also stand in solidarity with our fellow Mechistas, who are in struggle to permanently keep the Chicano mural on this campus as well as to increase the number of Chicano/Latino students on this campus. We will hold this university accountable to its mission statement: "UC San Diego embraces diversity, equity, and inclusion as essential ingredients of its academic excellence in higher education." We would like to stress that none of the following demands are new, and we will not be ignored anymore.

In this state of emergency, the Black Student Union, alongside our current student, faculty, and staff supporters and allies demand the following:

- Firstly, in regard to access to higher education for underrepresented students we demands permanent funding for student-initiated access programs. As a public institution, UCSD has a responsibility to the historically underrepresented communities that it should serve, on top of the fact that it has a Student-Promoted Access Center for Education and Service doing more than enough work in the field of access. SPACES is a student-run, student-initiated center, meaning that the STUDENTS are doing the work that the university should do.
- In regards to admissions, we demand that the admissions policy contin-ues as comprehensive review, with addition points given to first-genera-tion college students and students who attend a fourth- or fifth-quintile high school in California. The senate administration task force on budget proposed to increase non-residential enrollment by switching from a comprehensive review to a holistic review. We demand that half of the revenue generated from non-resident tuition be allocated to programs specifically designed to access, retention of underrepresented students of California at UC San Diego. We also demand that the university announce public plans to ensure that the pool admitted out-of-state students resembles the demographic of California.
- In regards to yield, we demand that the university begin to do its work in recruiting historically underrepresented students by implementing yield programs initiated by the students and fully funded by the university. Yield is designed to facilitate the transition between student-initiated access and student-initiated retention programs. This is solely the

responsibility of the university to fund, implement, and maintain such listed programs. It institutionalizes the efforts of recruitment to this campus by placing part of the responsibility in the hands of the administration.

- In regard to the retention of historically underrepresented and under-served students, we demand the necessary institutional resources for programs that contribute to our intellectual, socio-cultural development, retention and achievement. In addition to the Academic Success Program and the Student-Promoted Access Center for Education and Service, the community centers also provide internships to students, host events relevant to minority struggles, with a clear focus on validating the presence and contributions of underrepresented groups.

- In regards to academics, we demand strong institutional support for academic programs that contribute to and improve campus climate. We demand that the university establish organized research units to work toward supporting research of African American, Chicano, Native American, and indigenous communities.

- In regards to administrative accountability, we demand that UC San Diego administration take responsibility for implementing institutional action to develop and maintain a critical mass of underrepresented students. We demand the expansion of the Chief Diversity Officer to an Associate Vice Chancellor of Diversity Affairs as a full-time position, with a fully funded office, with a responsibility for all campus diversity initiatives. This person will not be responsible for the Preuss School. We demand that students from the Student Affirmative Action Committee to be participants in the search process.

- In regards to campus climate, we demand a climate that promotes and addresses the needs of historically underrepresented communities.

- Finally, we demand that the administration respond to these demands on March 4th, in a thorough written response with details on how each program will be implemented and a timeline for immediate action. The chancellor has had more than enough time these past few years to make a decision. We expect all of the administration to meet on library walk, Thursday, to state their measures on these demands, while allowing the students to respond back. As students, WE will set up the stage and speakers on library walk; we only ask that your presence is there, Chancellor Fox, Vice Chancellor of Student Affairs Penny Rue, all academic senators, all academic senate representatives, and all administration. If these demands are not addressed and decided upon, we as African American students and allies will be forced to send out a public call to other universities to provide us the educational environment free from degradation, hostility, and intimidation that the University of California, San Diego refuses to provide.

UCLA STUDENT ANDREA ORTEGA SPEAKS TO UCSD STUDENTS ON LIBRARY WALK

February 23, 2010

I'm Andrea Ortega, I'm a student at UCLA and I'm here in solidarity with the UCSD students, in solidarity with students of color across the country, and all the people marginalized in this world. This is really an issue that affects us all. Earlier this week, there is a group of students marching from Florida to Washington DC, to bring attention to the issue of undocumented students. And they reached Georgia, and they were confronted by the KKK, and there were so many racist comments, and it hurt.

So this week, at UCLA, I didn't sleep working to bring awareness on campus. But last night, when I heard about the noose so close to home, right here, in the library of UCSD, it hurt. It hurt so much! And to hear that they found the person who put the noose there, and he doesn't understand what he did?!? That's BULLSHIT! He should be right here—CONFRONTING THE CONSEQUENCES OF HIS ACTIONS!"

white girl from the o.c.
even the comments here are appalling and heartbreaking. i yearn for a world where people love more than they hurt. that party invite was incredibly offensive and the people who were involved should be thoroughly humbled rather than defensive. the people who were hurt by it... show the humility that others are to proud to display.
February 25, 2010, 5:18:58 PM PST – Flag – Like – Reply
Liked by Guest

HarryBalls
Tissues please for the underprivileged white girl. The Balls understands how hurt she must feel over this live changing event, boo hoo; he really does. This may well be the worst calamity she has ever faced. Is there a therapist following this thread who can offer some words of condolence or encouragement? Maybe something like, WTF?
February 26, 2010, 12:34:49 AM PST – Flag – Like – Reply

A Letter from Jody Blanco
Regarding Recent Events on Campus

February 21, 2010

Dear friends,
Please take the time to read the moving and necessary letter below, written by Jody Blanco, a professor in the Department of Literature, to the students of Kaibigang Pilipino (KP).
In solidarity,
j.

Dear Filipina and Filipino students, colleagues, and friends:

I hope that you don't mind my sending a mass email to you, which is something I don't think I've ever done. While I know some, maybe many of you individually, I haven't been to a KP GBM in many years, and haven't had the opportunity to work as closely with you as I would have liked and would like to. Hopefully this is something we can begin to address and repair over time.

What has prompted this unusual message is the recent spate of events that have transpired the past week, and have caused or exacerbated the perceived lack of support for many historically underrepresented minorities—not just blacks, but Latinos, Arab- and certain Asian-Americans, Filipinos and Filipino-Americans included. I don't need to tell you the details, which I'm sure you already know—a private party involving hundreds of UCSD students, framed as an expression of contempt for Black History Month and the free use of hate speech (which, as it turns out, was downloaded from a website); a follow-up televised program on the Koala newspaper website, expressing support for hate speech.

By now, if you've been listening to the local and national news, you may also have a sense of the fallout: black students at UCSD threatening to withdraw or transfer out of UCSD en masse; the administration's simultaneous condemnation of these events and declaration of non-commitment to any further significant actions to be taken in response to the outbreak of hate speech on campus; the intervention of the San Diego city council and California state assembly members committed to take responsibility and hold people accountable (because the university won't); a public statement made by the NAACP promising to conduct its own investigation into the matter; national coverage of our campus and university on network TV, featuring reporters and analysts who express open disbelief at the campus's presumed commitment to its principles of community, and bewilderment at the administration's failure to take any meaningful or effective action defending and protecting its students from injury and insult.

For those of you who have close friends in the black community, you may have witnessed or heard stories of their trauma and insecurity: students weeping in the halls and on Library Walk at their helplessness and inability to represent themselves against the violence of having other people represent them. If you are like me, you are familiar with this feeling: you have grown up seeing your parents scolded by an angry grocery clerk or policeman for appearing ignorant or slow; you have been denigrated or mocked by whites for excelling at the things you love or feel passionate about; you have felt betrayed by an authority who witnessed your persecution at one point or another, and pretended not to notice. You are familiar with the mistrust, lack of confidence, and sometimes, the outright fear, of the world outside your immediate family and friends;

you have struggled consciously or unconsciously to accept or refuse the possibility that the world outside this insulated circle neither values nor encourages your participation and contribution to a wider community. If you can't relate to what I'm saying, perhaps it's all for the best, because I wouldn't wish that consciousness and psychological conflict on anybody. But if you can relate to what your African-American brothers and sisters are feeling, you probably also understand that this is what most ethnic and / or historically underrepresented minorities, in the US and in every country, experience to one degree or another. It is the experience we share in common, an experience that oftentimes draws us close to one another in times of danger.

I want to underline this last point in order to foreground my basic message: I'm asking you to become or stay involved, and to make sure there are always Pinoy and Pinay voices, in the responses and activities

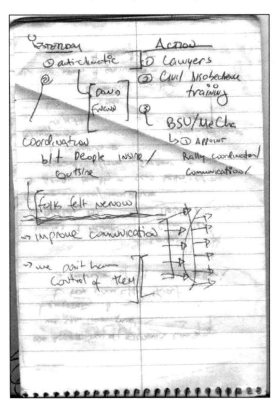

to this event that will occur in the following weeks or months. I'm asking you to become or stay involved, first and foremost, because as historically underrepresented minorities we are directly implicated in both acts of racial hate speech and the university's responses to it. As many of you who have taken my classes before may know, when the US conducted a near-genocidal war against the Philippines at the beginning of the twentieth century (which left between

500,000-1,000,000 dead, mostly civilians), both US soldiers and commanders often referred to Filipinos as "niggers." In the 1920s and 30s, when Filipino Carlos Bulosan and his compatriots came to the US to escape the US-driven poverty in the Philippines, they were identified as "niggers," and they were lynched, beaten, and murdered without any recourse to the law. To this day, the word retains the same popular meaning as it did at the turn of the century: to be a "nigger" means to be identified as an available target for extra-judicial violence and social exile, without right of appeal to an established or legitimate authority. This is what the word means, regardless of who uses it in what context. That is what makes it a dangerous word and concept. It is a word that attacks what it identifies, and paves the way for further violence.

My second reason for asking for your committed involvement is that your African-American friends, collaborators, and co-sponsors need you. They need you to defend and protect them, to promote and cultivate a climate and community that respects, safeguards, and enhances our humanity: our right to belong, to participate and contribute to the realization of common dreams. You may think that, because you don't have as many co-sponsored activities with BSU, MEChA, or APSA, you don't have much in common with them. You are wrong. We are all fighting to increase student recruitment and retention of historically underrepresented minorities at UCSD, whereas the groups that comprise the majorities at UCSD don't need to do this. We are all faced with constant underfunding and are obliged to conduct recruitment and retention activities that are regularly performed by hired full-time staff in most other universities. We are all passionately invested in reproducing and reinventing the originality of our cultural heritage, its joys and sorrows, which help us understand how and why we remain separate from a greater cultural heritage that might be simply defined as "American." They need you to give them respect, and ask for their respect in return. They need you to validate their humanity and their belonging; and to ask that they validate ours. They are our kababayan, whether they know it or not. In the past, African-Americans have historically fought for our rights to self-determination, both in the Philippines and in the United States. Whether we, or our parents, know it or not, we owe a great debt to them: both directly and indirectly, through the ways we have benefited from their pioneering struggles and sufferings. It is time to begin repaying that debt.

The third reason I ask for your concern and involvement is that it is time for our presence to be felt as a strong and united constituency within the UCSD academic community. Many of our parents raised us under the idea that if we wanted to pursue the American way of life, we have to shut up, avoid any negative attention, do our work quietly, respect all established authority, and pray that our efforts would be recognized and rewarded on earth as they would be in heaven. Our employers and managers tell us that our proper attitude towards authority should be a submissive form of gratitude. But to be a constituency means to actively participate in the constitution of governance, and one of the tasks of governance is the administration of justice. Have we been assigned the task and given the authority to act as judges over this case? No. Can our voices frame the way justice is administered, or imagined? As a constituency, yes.

A fourth and final reason for our support and involvement is that it gives us the opportunity to have the courage to use our own reason in the understanding and exploration of our racialized past and present. University administrators by and large have chosen to exonerate themselves from responsibility for the actions of the students and groups involved in these expressions of hate speech. Their reason for doing so, among others, is that they are afraid of legal repercussions if any reprisals implicate the university for infringing on the right to free speech, particularly when students are "technically" off campus.

In my opinion, this question does not rank as one of the more important questions to be asking about the implications of hate speech associated with our university. As Marx once said, the answer always depends on the form of the question that's being asked. Do the events of the past week all boil down to the question of whether or not students have the right to exercise free speech? No. The scandal isn't that the right to free speech might even include the right for individuals to denigrate and stereotype people: I can turn the TV to Fox News Channel and see the proof of that for myself any given day. The scandal is that an event like this could only happen in or around a university or institution that has failed in its commitment to academic and cultural diversity. The scandal is that many students at UCSD consider black people and communities as a product of their imaginations and consumer habits: an entertainment commodity we pay to watch on MTV, or hear on the radio. A stereotype we have the "right" to enjoy and take pleasure in, because we have paid good money to possess and consume it in the privacy of our homes and TV screens. The scandal is that many whites—and even Asian Americans—do not belong to a community that involved and involves the active participation and vital humanity of another person or community of color, another historically underrepresented minority. It's not hard to see why: only 1 of every 50 students on this campus is African American, and only 1 of 10 students is Latina / Latino.

As those of you involved in the recruitment and retention of Pinay / Pinoy students on campus must know, when you deny a person, or group the right and opportunity to be part of a community, you deprive that person or group of the opportunity to represent and express their humanity. The dehumanization involved in the promotion of stereotypes is just a surface expression of a deeper, systemic dehumanization that has taken place, and that continues to take place in our university. The tragedy is the system that allowed, and even promoted, the permanent exile of a group of human beings from any meaningful participation in any form of community in America.

What can we do to change this? That's my question. What's yours?

Thank you for your time and attention. If anyone is interested in talking to me about this letter or the events more broadly, feel free to email me (jdblanco@ucsd.edu) or pass by my office hours (Thursdays 10am-12pm) at the Cross Cultural Center.

Sumasainyo,
Jody Blanco, Department of Literature

Petition from UCSD's Faculty of African Descent

To: Faculty Colleagues, UCSD Administration and UC Regents

As faculty of African descent here at the University of California, San Diego, we write to express our disgust at the racist and misogynist events of last week. We hope that the students understand that we stand alongside them. We thank those colleagues who have contacted us individually and collectively to express their anger at the attitudes and behavior of the members of Pi Kappa Alpha and the Koala. We ask that the entire faculty join us in a demonstration of common outrage, and assist us in moving forward by signaling agreement with the ideas expressed in this statement.   As the undergraduate students have explained, both the "Compton Cookout" and the racist drivel broadcast on SR-TV are indicative of a broader campus climate of hostility and neglect. We believe that UC San Diego must act strongly, both to sanction appropriately those responsible for these events and, equally importantly, to augment our intellectual and personal commitment to confronting the problems of outreach, yield, and retention in respect to underrepresented communities in general—and African American students in particular—on our campus. We are proud of the many efforts made by dedicated faculty, students and staff across the campus aimed at fostering a more hospitable environment, improving yield, and producing curricular innovation. We share their fear of the devastating long-term effects that will result if this university acquires a national or international reputation for intolerance and bigotry.   We stand today at a crossroads. Addressing the academic and student affairs needs of historically underrepresented groups remains one of this

Photo courtesy of Erik Jepsen.

institution's most glaring areas of unfulfilled promise. In the previous decade, the university has convened a number of committees charged with improving admissions and undergraduate yield, faculty equity and diversity, and the larger climate and reputation of UCSD. We do not wish to see further duplication. We have had task forces: now we need resources. We understand that the university faces a profound financial crisis. Nevertheless, we believe that this crisis cannot become the rationale for any slackening of efforts in regard to racial and ethnic diversity, increased educational access, or the creation of a campus climate that accurately reflects the UCSD mission of the fullest possible access to education, research, and public service.   We ask our colleagues from across the campus to add their voices to ours by signing on to this letter.

Sincerely,
The Undersigned

View Signatures : 786   736   686   636   586   536   486   436   386   336   286   236   186
136   86   36

THEY'RE NOT TAKING THE STUDENTS OF THIS UNIVERSITY SERIOUSLY

Professor Daniel Widener and Fnann Keflegizhi
Address to the students occupying the Chancellor's complex,
February 26, 2010

Fnann: Hello everyone. So as you all know, we just got out of a meeting with Chancellor Fox. All those folks. And they handed us over a bullshit-ass document. Basically it said everything we already knew, no concrete things on how they're going to implement anything. So they're definitely dumber than we thought they were—a lot dumber than *I* thought they were. I mean, I thought they were going to pull it together today, but apparently not. I'm pretty pissed … .off right now. Clearly they're not taking us seriously. That's how I feel. I don't know how y'all feel. But they're not taking me seriously, they're not taking us seriously, and they're not taking the students of this university seriously …

Danny: Everybody, I know everyone has been out all day long I just wonder if we can take a minute to salute the students who have been here all day long, the ones who have been outside and the ones who have been inside. (cheers)
We have good news, and we have bad news. Which do you want first?

Crowd: BAD!

Prof. Widener: Well, the bad news is, the University gave us a—what was it you called the document?

Fnann: Bullshit-ass—

Prof. Widener: —document. You want to hear the good news?

Crowd: Yeah!
Prof. Widener: The University gave us a—what was it you called it?

Crowd: BULLSHIT!

Prof. Widener: —document. Okay, so that's what this means on a couple of levels. First, they've given us the work of creating a document that is specific, that is comprehensive, and that aims at creating a university where we feel respected, where we feel protected, and where we feel we have the possibility to succeed, whether we're freshmen, or tenured faculty.

We need help. And I want to just outline some of the process and then I hope that we can agree that everybody who was here today will be here on Monday, and that everybody who was here today will be prepared to bring one more person with them on Monday.

Just one more thing before we close, I want to point something out. From 8:00 this morning until now, the University operated on our timetable, on our schedule. And although they didn't' do the best job of coming back to us with something we could comprehend, something we could implement. Today we seized the heart of this place. Next week—Monday, Tuesday, Wednesday, Thursday, Friday—we come back to seize the heart, but we move out to seize the brain, the eyes, the lips, the teeth, the tongue, the feet, the arms, the legs, the whole thing!

As you heard from the alumni, this didn't begin with us, it won't end next week. We need to come together strongly, we need to push for what it is that everyone knows we need, what it is we want, which is, we felt REAL PAIN, we demand—

Crowd: REAL ACTION!

Photo courtesy of Erik Jepsen.

Legislators Denounce UCSD Racist Party

Perette Gordon, Fox5 *San Diego, February 19, 2010*

SACRAMENTO, Calif.—California state legislatures are demanding a swift investigation into the "Compton cookout" party planned by University of California San Diego students.

Members of the California state legislature held a news conference Thursday in regards to the "ghetto-themed" party that took place last weekend in San Diego. In the invitation, planners said they were throwing it to "honor black history month."

California Assemblyman who represents Compton, democratic representative for the 52nd district Isadore Hall III, spoke at the news conference. His district was satirized in the UCSD students' invitation.

"I stand here today united with fellow legislative leaders, in publicly condemning those responsible for these acts of hate," said Hall. "My constituents, people throughout California and across the nation, have contacted me sharing their outrage that here we are in 2010, during black history, college educated kids at one of the finest public universities in California could be responsible for such a hurtful and blatant act of racism, sexism and hate."

Hall described the invitation as hurtful and blatant racism, "It contained about every inflammatory, derogatory, racist and negative stereotype of African Americans that I can think of."

Members of San Diego's legislative contingent also spoke.

"Believe me, I am deeply saddened and angry that this is happened in San Diego, in my city," said Senator Christine Kehoe, the democratic representative for the 39th district. "I believe this kind of activity does not reflect the value and attitudes of San Diegans, or the UCSD community."

Invitations to the party were sent via the social networking site Facebook. Under the description, administrators referred to black history month and wrote, "in hopes of showing respect, you are invited to the first 'Compton Cookout'." Guys were asked to wear jerseys, Fubu, chains and other items. Women were asked to appear as "ghetto chicks" described as wearing gold teeth, bad weaves, nappy hair and talking loud.

The University is conducting an investigation into the party, amid allegations that it was thrown by fraternities associated with the school.

"I don't want these organizations to merely apologize for their actions, I want names," said Hall. "I want these individuals and these organizations to understand that this racist and sexist behavior will not be tolerated here in California."

One of the fraternities alleged to be involved, Pi Kappa Alpha (Pike), has issued a statement on its website. In it, the president said his organizations was not involved and apologized for the display of ignorance and error-of-judgment made by any individual members who may have attended. Of the four boys whose names appear under the admin section of the invitation, one is a member of Pike. Another is a member of Sigma Nu fraternity.

University administrators are planning a 2-hour teach-in for next week and plans for a "Not in our Community" campaign. Compton's assemblyman said it is not enough.

"We sit in history classes all day at the University," said Hall. "We have teach-ins every single day. We need action and we're not going to band aid this by having a sit-in."

Interfaith Rose Response Statement

Chancellor's complex occupation, March 1, 2010

This is March 1, 2010. This morning, in response to the act of racial terror that took place on campus last Thursday, the members of the UCSD Catholic Community, the Newman Center, the Muslim Student Association of UCSD, and students of other faith traditions, took action to reclaim Geisel Library. More than 40 students entered the 7th floor, and filled it with roses of all colors, representing the beautiful diversity of the UCSD student population, and affirming the right of each one of us to study in peace and safety in our library.

We ask you to stop by the 7th floor of Geisel Library before 5 pm today, and pick up one of these roses.

We ask that you carry it with you to show your support for the BSU, and other students that are working for equality and social justice at UC-San Diego.

Posted in the library is this statement:

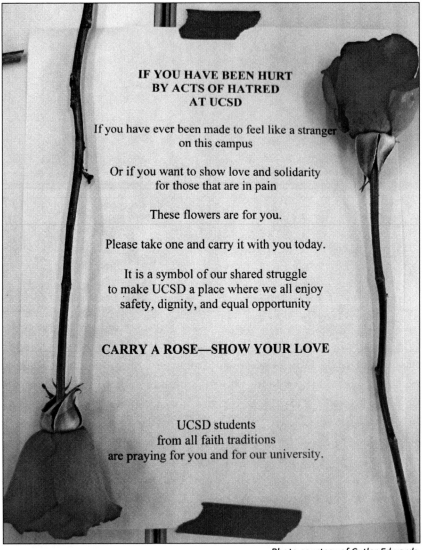

**IF YOU HAVE BEEN HURT
BY ACTS OF HATRED
AT UCSD**

If you have ever been made to feel like a stranger
on this campus

Or if you want to show love and solidarity
for those that are in pain

These flowers are for you.

Please take one and carry it with you today.

It is a symbol of our shared struggle
to make UCSD a place where we all enjoy
safety, dignity, and equal opportunity

CARRY A ROSE—SHOW YOUR LOVE

UCSD students
from all faith traditions
are praying for you and for our university.

Photo courtesy of Cutler Edwards.

Micha Cardenas Speaks at Chancellor's Complex Occupation

March 1, 2010

...We all share in this struggle. So, I just want to put this out there, and ask everybody who's here now: Is it really okay if the administration accepts ALL of the BSU's demands, and we're all just going to go home and be happy, and then come back on Thursday, and have a *new* set of demands? That seems really—curious, I think—I don't really understand that. I guess my question is, maybe I should propose to everybody, that we can consider, that maybe we should stay here until they meet the BSU demands, AND all the March 4th demands AND they close the Literature Building?

Because how is it okay if they meet all the BSU demands, but then Literature professors are dying of cancer, and then after Thursday people are still getting fired, and losing their jobs?

That doesn't make any sense.

So what I really wanted to say, is since we're all here together, is that maybe we should think about how we can make this OUR space. Right? It's not the chancellor's complex, it's our space. And it's our time. And maybe we could, you know, talk amongst ourselves, and decide if that's something we want to do. Thanks.

Photo courtesy of Erik Jepsen.

ISULONG: AN OPEN LETTER TO OUR MGA KASAMA HERE AT THE UNIVERSITY OF CALIFORNIA, SAN DIEGO

February 28, 2010

Dear Sisters and Brothers of BSU and MEChA:

We, Kamalayan Kollective, a political, people-centered, feminist organization here at UCSD, stand in solidarity with you in your brave efforts to create a just and lasting institutional change at our university. Your recent mobilizations on our campus in response to the explicit acts of racism and the administration's failure to address adequately your demands prove the intelligence and resilience of students of color and our unwavering commitment to actualized social and educational justice. We do not merely applaud your efforts, rather, we raise our fists and march with you, for we, as Filipina/o students, have, always have had, and always will have your back.

As a decolonizing people, we hold dear and work diligently on the premise that we have inherited a revolutionary legacy of working across community identities. During the 1950's, the Filipino farm workers struggled alongside our Chicana/o sisters and brothers in the United Farm Workers Movement; Filipina/o activists linked arms with our sisters and brothers of color in order to push for civil rights, in order to push for the demands of Black, Brown, Yellow and Red Power movements. At the turn of the century, Black soldiers during the Philippine-American War defected from the U.S. Army in order to fight for Philippine independence. The Latina/o community and the Filipina/o community have come together on multiple occasions to resist the anti-immigrant character of our campus and this country. In all acts of self-determination, we undoubtedly have had your back and you undoubtedly have had ours.

More pertinently, on this campus, we, as Filipina/o students, who make up a mere 4% of the undergraduate population, who continue to experience the effects of institutional neglect, resist the cultures of racism, sexism, classism, and homophobia. We are pained to witness our sisters and brothers in the local San Diego Filipina/o American community shut out of this institution, and instead exploited for cheap labor and tracked into the military and into prisons. Through these conditions, we emerge as leaders behind significant campus projects and community campaigns such as SIORC, SPACES, the Justice for Janitors Campaign, and campaigns for Affirmative Action. We initiate long-term and short-term projects to eradicate the ills of imperialism, racism, misogyny, classism, sexism, and homophobia on this campus. We have developed (with minimal to no help from the University) our own spaces such as Pinay Speaks, Pinayism Class (2005, 2007, 2010) and several other Directed Group Studies courses in order to confront the toxicity of this campus and to acknowledge that real pain and real oppression also exists along the horizontal axes of social category. We draw upon this legacy as radical Filipina/o organizers in the United States in order to identify ourselves not as allies to your Movement, but as comrades and comadres in the same struggle.

We, Kamalayan Kollective, are here to have your back. As under-served students directly affected and traumatized by the campus climate, we are taking a stand in representing the voice of the Filipina/o students who are in solidarity with you. We continue to believe in the necessity of real and immediate action. Sisters and brothers, in these times of struggle, we need you to have our back as much as you need us to have yours. Together, we do more than stand, we fight! MAKIBAKA! HUWAG MATAKOT!

Real Pain, Real Action, Isang Bagsak, Isang Mahal,
Kamalayan Kollective

Letter of Support and Solidarity to UCSD Black Student Union

From UC Berkeley's APIEL NOW!, March 1, 2010

To the UCSD Black Student Union and their allies:

We, the members of Asian Pacific Islander Education and Languages NOW! (APIEL NOW!) at UC Berkeley, are outraged by the racist, hostile, and demoralizing events that have transpired over the past two weeks at UC San Diego. We stand in full solidarity with your struggle to push the UCSD administration both to change its institutionalized practices of racism, classism, sexism, and homophobia and to commit to creating a safe and empowering living and learning environment for the African-American community and other historically underrepresented communities of color on campus.

Far from being isolated incidents of racism at UCSD that can be addressed through teach-ins, the "Compton Cookout," the racially derogatory comments made by SR-TV, and the noose found hanging in the UCSD library collectively point to the deeper problems of institutional racism and marginalization both within and outside of the education system that perpetuate these kind of ignorant and hateful acts. In a joint statement, the UC President and the Chancellors condemn the racist incidents and state that they "reflect neither our principles nor the values, nor the sentiments of the University of California community," yet it is clear to all communities of color that condemnation alone does not create real change, nor does it begin to address the real root of the problem: the continued segregation of public schools; the lack of stable and fully-funded resources to recruit, retain, and support students of color in all levels of education; the repeated division of labor along racial, gender, and class lines; the barriers that continually deny underrepresented communities access to public services such as affordable health care, decent housing, stable jobs, decent working conditions, and adequate representation; and the failure of the educational system to build awareness about and to teach students about racism, classism, sexism, homophobia, and the need for affirmative action.

We in APIEL NOW! recognize that the fight communities of color face in higher education is against an administration that neither prioritizes students, faculty and workers of color, nor is willing to transform the higher education system into one that actually acknowledges and actively seek to *fight* the daily oppression and exclusion that underrepresented communities of color face. We are outraged that even though African American students make up only 1.3% of the student population at UCSD, the UC administration still plans to implement a new admissions policy in 2012 that will effectively decrease the number of African American students previously eligible for guaranteed admission to UC by nearly 50%. "Representation" and "diversity" at the UC are both empty terms. Having representation from historically underrepresented communities on a campus does not mean that they are equal, nor does it mean that their peers will automatically have, and more importantly, *practice* a critical understanding of the history of violence, repression, and exclusion that underrepresented communities face on a daily basis.

We fully support the demands that you have raised, all of which point to key ways to build permanent and institutionally-supported classes, programs, support services (academic, emotional, financial), and spaces that will create a welcoming campus climate and learning environment actively shaped by the African American community's and historically underrepresented ethnic communities' concerns and demands.

We stand behind your demand that UCSD better educate the campus about underrepresented communities' histories through mandated diversity sensitivity requirements in African-American Studies, Ethnic Studies, and Gender Studies, and we hope that the university will develop these departments so they have the breadth and depth necessary to give students a *comprehensive* understanding of the struggles that underrepresented communities of color face in a society that is still fundamentally divided and racist. The budget cuts are no excuse for not making immediate changes to a deeply flawed curriculum and educational system. The San Francisco Unified School District, for example, where 90% of the K-12 students are nonwhite, just approved a pilot program last week that will add Ethic Studies classes to their high school curriculum. Alongside UCSD BSU, we will continue to fight to make Ethnic Studies, African-American Studies, Gender and Woman Studies, Chicana/o Latina/o Studies, Native American Studies, Middle-Eastern Studies, Asian Pacific Islander American Studies, and South/Southeast Asian Studies an integral part of every K-UC school.

Today, we watched the Black community at UC Berkeley stand in front of Sather Gate for two-and-a-half hours in silent solidarity with you and pass out literature to the rest of the student body—literature that documented both the acts of hatred that took place at UCSD, as well as every racist incident that has taken place against the Black community at UC Berkeley for the past nine years. Next Monday, we will stand in solidarity at Sather Gate with you and with them when they hold their second nonviolent, silent demonstration at Sather Gate. We are ready to help in whatever way we can to fight for the rights of those in our communities who have been marginalized and oppressed.

In solidarity and struggle,
Asian Pacific Islander Education and Languages NOW!
UC Berkeley

Photo courtesy of Curtis Marez.

SOLIDARITY FROM THE SCIENTIFIC COMMUNITY AT UCSD

This letter was sent to Chancellor Fox from community members in the Scripps Oceanography Institute.

Chancellor Fox,

We, the community of Scripps Institution of Oceanography at UCSD, will not tolerate racism or hate at our school. This institution is a place of higher learning for people of all ethnicities, socioeconomic standings, genders, religions, and sexual orientations. Brilliance knows none of these boundaries, and we actively reject discrimination based on any of these personal identifying backgrounds. The purpose of this letter is to unite SIO in support of the individuals who feel hurt by recent racist acts, and to ask that administrators recognize the need to actively mend the rifts these acts have highlighted.

The February 2010 acts of individual members of the UCSD community involving the racially offensive "Compton cookout", the use of the "N" word on the student-run TV station by the Koala, and the display of the noose at Geisel Library are divisive and abhorrent. These individuals' ignorance, gross insensitivity, and hatefulness have no place at UCSD.

Intellectual communities, like social communities, are enriched and stimulated by diversity. As we strive for the best intellectual environment at our institution, we recognize that we must fight for the inclusion and protection of underrepresented groups. We embrace these groups and value their contributions to our community. We will absolutely not accept threats and hate towards them. Furthermore, as members of the SIO community, we recognize that in our position of privilege, it is unethical to fail to defend minority groups that are abused by members of the majority. We will not stand for it. Not in our community.

Too often, SIO is cloaked in apathy owing in part to its physical separation from both the main UCSD campus and less privileged areas of San Diego. Today, however, we take action. We come together to support diversity and justice. We are committed to those who feel emotionally burdened by recent events and who struggle to fulfill their duties both to research and to our hurting community. We are also committed to the underrepresented groups that already reside at our institution, and we are fighting to retain them in an atmosphere that is welcoming to all individuals.

The current friction on campus affects far more than the 2% of students directly targeted by the hateful acts. It affects all students, faculty, and staff members who value our community. By signing this letter, we are supporting our classmates and colleagues, both at SIO and on upper campus, pledging "Not in our community!" We will stand against hate and insist on administrative action to improve the campus climate. We will listen to the concerns and fears of our classmates and colleagues, and dedicate the necessary time and resources to mend our fractured campus. Together we promote compassion, empathy, respect, and intellectual exchange for all members of our community.

Thanks and Peace,
Proud Advocates for a Diverse and Inclusive UCSD and SIO

Enrique De La Cruz, Colectivo Zapatista San Diego, Speaks in Support at Friday Morning Rally

February 26, 2010

Good morning, Buenos Dias. Mi nombre es Enrique de la Cruz and I'm with Colectivo Zapatista San Diego, it's a community organization in San Diego. Just really quick here, just to let you know that you're not alone.

The text thing is crazy, this morning I got a text, I woke up and I was sleeping, estaba dormido, and I was like "no se", then I was like "oh shit, it's says n*oose*." I was like, "It's a noose!"

But real quick, props to you, just to let you know that students, whatever, with parents and everybody, some of us are with the Centro Cultural de la Raza in Balboa Park and that's a space that's going thru current struggles right now. That's a space that we're fighting for not to become all corporate and shit. Really, keep fighting because like the compas were saying, if you don't fight now it could get worst, we won't have anything to fight for later on.

Really quick, the Zapatistas have a saying that says, "Su Lucha es Nuestra Lucha," y la lucha continua and the struggle continues. I just hear right now that the chancellor wants to speak or whatever, they

---

can wait like everybody else. On the real though, everybody says to be polite, in all honesty you can be organized and not be polite. I have to be around and be like, "sorry." I'm like, "fuck that." People judge me when I speak and I'm like. "fuck that, man."

Really, keep it going and we'll be with you. People in San Diego, people in Mission Bay know, even PB Middle School knows already, they're like, "Damn!"

Announcement of Matched Funding During Occupation of Chancellor's Complex

Desiree Prevo, March 1, 2010

We got our funding matched with SPACES, SHAPES, and the ASP programs, by the University, so congratulations!

Photo courtesy of Erik Jepsen.

University of San Diego Women of Color Statement

Adriana Secord, Alyssa Crow and C. Marie Holloway

Rachel Gasca

As women of color at the University of San Diego, we are outraged and saddened by the events and actions of the students involved in the "Compton Cookout" from the University of California San Diego. This is not merely a disappointment in the implicated fraternities, but also in any other persons who planned or attended this event. To those students who were affected by this disgusting display of racism, know that members of the USD community support you. An injustice to one is an injustice to all.

Incidents like this confirm that the legacy of American colonialism still pervades our everyday lives. White supremacy and heteronormativity, built on the backs of people of color and low-wage labor, are the standards by which social structures are constituted and passed down to the next generation. The party that was meant to be a lighthearted event parallels 20th-century lynching parties where throngs of people would congregate to lynch one or more African-Americans and then proceed to feast and BBQ.

It is a mockery, an attraction created for the socially and politically protected so that poverty and racism are no longer real and viable issues; instead they have become themes for parties of the privileged. This heinous disregard for the plight of people living in impoverished communities justifies their continued dehumanization. The students who took part, whether they organized or attended this racist, heterosexist, classist party, must be held accountable for their actions and make a public apology for this inexcusable gathering. We call for this to be an educational moment on the themes of self-definition and community self-determination because, in the words of Malcolm X, "Without education, you're not going anywhere in this world." We stand in solidarity with UCSD's Black Student Union and support its important demands.

ADRIANA SECORD

ALYSSA CROW

C. MARIE HOLLOWAY

Photo courtesy of Cutler Edwards.

Students Walk Out of UC San Diego Teach-In

Larry Gordon, Los Angeles Times, *February 25, 2010*

The event was held in response to two recent racial incidents. But minority students don't believe the university will take significant steps to boost their numbers or improve conditions, one said.

A student walkout Wednesday disrupted a UC San Diego teach-in that was intended to promote tolerance in the wake of two recent racially charged incidents. Many of those involved said the protest showed how difficult it will be for the beachside campus to overcome long-standing concerns about the small number of African American students enrolled there.

More than 1,200 students, faculty and staff packed an auditorium in the student center for the teach-in, which campus administrators organized in response to the incidents, including an off-campus party Feb. 15 that mocked Black History Month.

But halfway through the planned two-hour session, hundreds of students walked out.

The students, who were joined by many others during the afternoon, held their own noisy but peaceful rally outside the building, calling on UC San Diego leaders to improve conditions for minority students and boost their numbers.

Administrators may have thought the teach-in "would make us quiet," said Fnann Keflezighi, vice chairwoman of the Black Student Union. But she said minority students do not believe that the university will take significant steps to improve the situation. The controversial party, she and others contended, was just the spark that ignited long-simmering ethnic tensions on the campus.

According to UC systemwide data, UC San Diego enrolled the smallest number of black freshmen last fall of any of the nine undergraduate campuses, 46 students out of a class of 3,749. Overall, officials say, about 1.6% of the campus' 23,143 undergraduates are African American, among the lowest percentages in the UC system.

On Wednesday, many students wore black and white T-shirts—"Real Pain, Real Action, 1.3%"—that noted the low enrollment figures, although with a slightly different calculation.

The teach-in moderator, Mentha Hynes-Wilson, an African American who is dean of students at UCSD's Thurgood Marshall College, went forward with the session for several hundred people who remained in the room after the walkout.

Hynes-Wilson said she was not offended by the disruption.

"That's what they needed to do, and we need to honor that," she said.

No one was arrested during the day of protests, and there were no reports of property damage, according to a campus spokesperson.

UCSD Chancellor Marye Anne Fox, who has condemned the off-campus "Compton Cookout," attended the teach-in but did not speak publicly. Administrators have said the campus is taking many steps within the law to boost recruitment of African American students and to provide more counseling and security on campus.

The university is also investigating whether it can discipline the organizers of the party, which promised guests a taste of "life in the ghetto."

The negative depiction of Compton has also upset residents of that city. To help counter those images, three teachers from Compton High School traveled to San

Diego on Wednesday and presented a statement from their students.

The statement, read by a Compton High graduate who is now a UCSD student, said that Latinos constitute 65% of Compton's population and that Latinos were also offended by the party.

"We are not going to sit idly by and watch our young people characterized as 'thugs' and 'ghetto chicks' by those who most likely have never been to our town," it said. "Learn about what you speak of before casting us in such a demeaning light."

Thomas Horne, an English teacher at Compton High, said students there who recently applied to UC campuses are now undecided about whether to attend UC San Diego. Some may be scared off by recent events, but others may be motivated to help boost the ranks of minority students there. "Where there is injustice, it encourages one or two to become that barrier breaker," he said.

Several days after the La Jolla party, racial tensions rose again when a campus satire group voiced support for the party and used a racial slur on a student television show.

The student-run station has been temporarily suspended, as has student government funding for some other publications.

About 300 students held a rally before Wednesday's teach-in, at which David Ritcherson, Black Student Union chairman, declared "a state of emergency to address the hostile and toxic environment on campus." He demanded that administrators increase funding for minority student recruitment and academic support beyond what Fox promised and said students who are in the first generation of their families to attend college should be given some preferences in admissions decisions.

But some had a different view.

Inez Feltscher, a UCSD student who heads the campus College Republicans club and participated in the teach-in, said she deplored the racially themed party but worried that the subsequent protests could deepen racial separation on the campus.

Feltscher, who called UCSD an "extreme leftist" school, said she was concerned that the recent events could reinforce an atmosphere of political correctness on campus.

Statement by UCSD's Department of Ethnic Studies

As faculty and graduate students in the Ethnic Studies Department at UC-San Diego, we unequivocally condemn the February 15th off-campus party, dubbed the "Compton Cookout," as an example of racist, classist and misogynist stereotyping that degrades Black people through disparaging representations of so-called "African American culture." Like similar events thrown on college and university campuses across the United States, this "theme party" in one quick, broad stroke reduced the complex lived experience of a heterogeneous racialized community to a caricatured depiction of cultural deviancy. All the more troubling, this particular themed party was intentionally organized to mock ongoing celebrations of African American History month in the U.S. and specifically here at UC San Diego.

This "monstrosity" (as some of the organizers called it) has a violent and racist history that began with blackface minstrel shows in the U.S., starting in the early 19th century, heightening with popularity during the Abolition Movement, and extending into 20th century theater and film. Both blackface minstrel performances and parties such as the "Compton Cookout" reinforce and magnify existing material and discursive structures of Black oppression, while denying Black people any sense of humanity, negating not only the actual lives that exist behind these caricatured performances but the structural conditions that shape Black life in the US. Far from celebrating Black history, events such as this one are marked celebrations of the play of power characteristic of whiteness in general and white minstrelsy in particular: the ability to move in and move out of a racially produced space at will; the capacity to embody a presumed deviance without actually ever becoming or being it; the privilege to revel in this raced and gendered alterity without ever having to question or encounter the systemic and epistemic violence that produces hierarchies of difference in the first place. Moreover, like their blackface minstrel predecessors, the organizers and attendees of the "Compton Cookout" demonstrate the inextricability of performances of white mastery over Black bodies from structures of patriarchy: by instructing their women 'guests' on how to dress ("wear cheap clothes"), behave ("start fights and drama"), and speak ("have a very limited vocabulary"), these young men not only paint a degrading and dehumanizing picture of African American women as so-called "ghetto chicks," but offer a recipe for the objectification of all women—made permissible, once again, through the appropriation of blackness.

Contrary to what some have claimed, the recent "Compton Cookout" is neither an aberration nor unique. Rather, it is best understood as part of a broader social reality that despite the celebrated juridical/political advancements achieved by people of color in the United States through centuries of struggle, full racial justice remains a goal, rather than accomplishment. The same month that we witnessed Barack Obama sworn in as the first Black man to reach the White House, the number of Black men imprisoned in the United States reached one million. Meanwhile, the backlash against affirmative action in public institutions that began a decade ago in the state of California has reduced representation of people of color in institutions ranging from the University of Michigan Law School to the New Haven Fire Department to public school districts across the US, making the criminal justice system the only state institution in which African Americans are still sought after and included in large numbers. Indeed, the unacknowledged slow reversal of the promise of Brown v. Board of Education is evident here at UCSD: Black students currently represent less than 2% of the undergraduate population here at UC San Diego, a percentage that is scarcely better than the 1% representation of Black people among faculty and academic professionals. Given this, despite the protestations of its organizers, events like the "Compton Cookout" are never "harmless fun." Rather, they are the cultural matter through which raced and gendered hierarchies of difference are reproduced and instantiated; they are the venues in which white privilege is rationalized through the representation of African Americans as less civilized and more deviant, less human and more animalistic, less deserving of education and more worthy of satire.

Indeed, the "Compton Cookout" demonstrates that as a country and as a campus, we have yet to create the institutional systems that would make places of higher education more accessible to and less alienating for Black students and other students of color. Indeed, if recent events on campus are any indicator, as a campus, we have only begun the work of recognizing our own complicities in the problem at hand. As scholars of race and power in the United States and transnationally, the faculty and students of the Ethnic Studies Department and our affiliates are well-versed in the history and intersectional analysis of events such as this recent party, and the continuing raced, classed, and gendered structures of inequality that it represents. We remain ready to assist the administration in not only developing "teach-ins" but also institutional policies capable of radically changing the campus climate within which such events can be conceived of as 'harmless' and be carried out unchecked.

In that vein, the Department of Ethnic Studies calls upon the University of California, San Diego administration to view this event not as an incident of wayward students violating the principles of UCSD's community, but rather to engage this event as a moment to re-think the logic of institutional accountability: who is responsible for creating a campus climate of permissibility around racial/gendered representational violence, and who pays the price of such a climate? We applaud the intellectual, political, and emotional work that is already being done by students, faculty and staff around the party and the broader issues it points to; at the same time, we recognize that moments such as this place additional and exhausting demands on a limited number of bodies, in part due to administrative expectations that students, faculty, and staff of color will serve as educators and crisis-managers, counselors and public representatives of the University. We therefore call upon the administration to model institutional accountability at the highest levels by taking concrete steps to make UCSD the educational and social environment promised by the Principles of Community—a university that is not only accessible to and affordable for African Americans and other students of color, but one in which students of color can feel valued, safe, and protected.

Photo courtesy of Minh Bui.

Petition from UC Community Members of Asian Descent

We the undersigned, UC community members (alumni, faculty, students and staff) of Asian descent, stand in solidarity with all who are protesting the racist incidents at UCSD and, more importantly, the systemic forces that support such incidents. It is unacceptable for UC campuses to view the recruitment and support of black and especially African-American students as anything other than a top priority. UCSD should never have allowed its black student population to languish at 1.6% of the total student population and ought to have paid much better attention to students' needs. The UC systemwide must take immediate and material action to improve the campus environments. We write as community members of Asian descent because we think it is particularly important for black students to know that they are supported by the group that is demographically the largest of the U.S. ethnic minority groups represented on UC campuses. We have common values and needs, and possess a history of African-American/Asian-American collaboration to draw upon, although this history is little publicized in the mainstream media. For example, African-Americans criticized anti-Chinese immigrant persecution in the late nineteenth century, and the Asian-American "yellow power" movement of the 1960's worked in solidarity with African-American movements toward common goals. We call upon these traditions, together with a sense of urgency that is only commensurate to a society that has effectively abandoned the pursuit of social justice, and pledge to stand with black students in their time of need.

David Ritcherson Speaks to Crowd Occupying the Chancellor's Complex

March 1, 2010

Can everybody hear me? What went down in there is we got a chance to explain to UCSD leadership, all the important decision-makers, *our* side of the story, where we're coming from. From the looks of things, everybody *says* they're in support and they want to work with us—you know how THAT goes—but everybody seems to be on the same page, about where we stand as far as our demands go, and how we want to see institutional change from this university. So you can clap it up for that shit!

But I also want to take this time to respect the space, and respect the opportunity we do have with the administrators. In there is going to be a crucial work-session, all the people that are going to be involved in the demands, in making institutional change, who are going to work with the students and the faculty, are all sitting in this room.

So we're going to have a real tight meeting, hopefully, and come out of there with things in writing, saying "this is going to be implemented," with a timeline. Real specific. So that's what we hope to see out of this meeting.

In the meantime, we're going to keep everybody out here energized, keep everybody updated on what's going on. We'd like to give some of the members of the Black Student Union an opportunity to explain the demands, go through the demands, so that people can ask questions about what's going on.

There are a lot of myths out there, lot of people *against* what we're trying to do … So we want to dispel some of those myths, and educate people on why we're here.

It's not just a black issue. It's not just a students of color issue. It's a *campus-wide* issue. [applause and cheers]

So we're going to go in here for about 30, 45 minutes, but I'll probably be peeking my head out to make sure everything's cool, everything's good. Is that cool?

Crowd: YEEEAAAAHHHH!!!!

HOLLA BACK! I GOT YOUR BACK!
HOLLA BACK! I GOT YOUR BACK!
HOLLA BACK! I GOT YOUR BACK!
HOLLA BACK! I GOT YOUR BACK!

Graduate Student Statement: Call for Successful Completion of Winter Quarter 2010

February 23, 2010

To the UCSD Campus Community:

There are three sides to the current state of emergency that has been declared—but not initiated—by students of color and their allies at UCSD:

(1) The first are those students of color and their allies who face the difficult and unwanted task of legitimizing and articulating their trauma in light of the current racist activity on and off campus;

(2) the second are the defenders of a status quo that excludes black students and trivializes their response to the recent racist actions on and off campus;

(3) the third group consists of a student body, faculty, and administration uncertain about what side to take and how far to go in their response to the current crisis.

We are not concerned with the second group here. Those defenders of the status quo have a fairly predictable task. As defenders of an entrenched hegemonic order, they have a safe and privileged role to perform in the current crisis: they will continue to hide behind legal rights, such as free speech, to justify actions and rhetoric that prolongs a long history of racism in which black culture and heritage is treated as their private property. They do not deserve our attention here because they feed on negative press and the further incitement toward controversy. This letter, rather, is written in alliance with the first group. Our demands are aimed at the UCSD administration and those members of the third audience who face the current situation at UCSD and who have a choice. We, the undersigned graduate students, occupy a somewhat removed vantage point on campus life, but that does not preclude us from making demands in alliance with our black brothers and sisters. We are teachers, students, and friends of undergraduate and graduate students of color. In these roles, we have seen the burden that is now placed on black students and their allies as they try to legitimize their feelings to an audience who is confused about the problem and its associated discussions. With scant resources and limited mentors on the UCSD campus, the marginalized 1.3 % and their allies have an enormous weight to carry. Even as we write, this unwanted weight is taking its emotional, academic, and physical toll on these students. Black students and their allies face the disproportionate task of balancing their academic work and social lives with the real radical demand to articulate their experience in a racialized environment. In the context of this state of emergency, the need to articulate their experience has become their main priority. They must miss classes. Their work must suffer. They must stay up for nights on end strategizing together as an excluded and unwanted community rather than studying as peers. While taking this necessary action in the name of their academic and human rights, they face the threat of physical and psychic assault from the campus community. They face the fear that their experiences are not legitimate in the eyes of their peers, teachers, and the administration. More distressingly, they face physical threats from supremacist groups and individuals on campus.

In light of these demands placed on black students and other students of color, we ask that the following demands be met this quarter:

- Counseling for students affected by the current state of emergency: We ask for the temporary hiring of more counseling staff, particularly black counselors, who can speak with students who face the emotionally and physically draining task of articulating their situation.
- Extensions on all academic work: Students who are struggling with the radical burden of articulating their experience cannot be academically penalized. If students are academically punished for their actions in the current state of emergency, we will consider it a form of racial violence enacted on the part of the administration.

- Classroom autonomy: Graduate students who elect to speak about these issues and the March 4th Day of Action should not be prevented from or penalized for taking a stance, regardless of the official position of the program.
- Creation of a pool of resources at the Center for Teaching Development: Undergraduate and graduate students from a wide variety of disciplines, regardless of whether they work as Teaching Assistants, need to have access to reference materials to use to facilitate productive discussions in the classroom about these issues.

Our purpose here is to intervene and implement changes in the short term for the successful completion of winter quarter, addressing specific needs we see in our capacity as graduate students who also work as Teaching Assistants on campus.

We are also in solidarity with the long-term demands made by the Black Student Union, Department of Ethnic Studies, and other letters that have been published. We are greatly inspired by the mobilization of our undergraduate students and look forward to the realization of these changes that have been demanded.

Sincerely,
Concerned Graduate Students and Teaching Assistants

Statement by UCSD Critical Gender Studies Faculty

Dear CGS Friends,

As concerned faculty affiliated with an academic program dedicated to the study of gender and sexuality at the intersections of class, race, ethnicity, religion, and other important organizing constructs of modern societies, we write to express our unequivocal support of the letter issued by the University of California, San Diego faculty of African descent, and ask that the University act immediately to respond to the demands by the Black Student Union.

We believe the racist and misogynist event last week is not an aberration but symptomatic of a larger systemic problem on our campus that the university has historically failed to redress. UCSD has not been forthcoming in fostering an intellectual and pedagogical environment hospitable to those who consider campus diversity foundational to teaching, critical thinking, research and public service. In the past this reticence has profoundly hampered our program's growth.

Over the past two decades, many faculty affiliated with the Critical Gender Studies Program (formerly Women's Studies Program) have dedicated their time and energy to increasing diversity on campus. In the absence of the University's commitment to supporting and sustaining historically underrepresented groups in general, and women of color in particular, an alarming number of African American and other CGS faculty of color have left the campus in bitter disappointment. An African American CGS faculty who recently left UCSD would lament that in her "Black Feminist Theory" class, she was the only "black feminist" in the room. Another African American CGS faculty, who published an award-winning book in timely fashion, was not tenured due to institutional oversight. She left UCSD to teach at a prestigious university with tenure. Earlier when a large number of CGS faculty were involved in the Coalition Against Segregation in Education (CASE) that rallied against the California's Proposition 209 under the banner, "No University without Diversity," the University neglected to publicly issue its commitment to diversity in education. After the offensive campus incident last week and the continuing acts of antagonism, we are now being asked to reach out to the prospective students from historically underrepresented communities to assure them that the recent display of hostility is not representative of UCSD. But some of us have been struggling against these conditions long enough to know that this is hardly unusual. At the same time, as faculty affiliated with a program that has managed to grow despite these serious setbacks, we are also aware that much can be accomplished with the concerted efforts and commitment of our students, staff and faculty mobilized for the consistent administrative leadership.

As faculty teaching in CGS, we are keenly aware of the intersecting oppressions many UCSD students face on a daily basis and we know how important it is to have programs like ours, giving all students the theoretical tools to analyze and challenge these structures. There are too few spaces on this campus that offer safety and support in an often alienating climate and we want to emphasize the amazing work done by the Cross Cultural, LGBTR and Women's Centers. These centers were created due to student pressure and the recent events show how important they and their commitment to intersectional politics still are. We are proud, though not surprised, that again students are taking the lead in pushing for a livable campus climate for all and we fully support their demands.

Symbolic gestures disavowing racism and misogyny will not usher in the changes necessary to achieve our highest aspirations in public education. The CGS Program faculty invites the entire campus community to support the University in its effort to implement the demands of our students and colleagues and immediately commit concrete institutional resources towards bringing forth substantial structural changes to UCSD.

Lisa Yoneyama, Director

Steering Committee:

Patrick Anderson, Communication
Fatima El-Tayeb, Literature
Sara Clarke Kaplan, Ethnic Studies/CGS
Nayan Shah, History

Distortion

Maria Teresa Ceseña, recited before a crowd of beautiful people demanding to be heard, February 26, 2010

U.S. frames cut my head from the picture
Our hands and our backs built the salad, no victors
Organic produce all the rage
Why weren't you enraged when my grandma touched those chemicals?

A table bused
A late-ass bus
Gangbangers push my gramma down waiting for the bus
Grab her purse that she bought at la pulga

No cash except bus fare
Still treasure was lost
First photos of babies
No diamonds, no watch

Su dignidad down
On a sidewalk that crumbles
When the earth quakes
We crash and stumble
For words and for actions
That could set us all free

Our thoughts, our reactions
We all gotta be
Open to the silence
That renders obsolete
These frames that cut my head off
Distort my mouth and feet

Foreign bodies that didn't matter
Dreams deferred, we got fatter
But we still have a voice
If only we could listen

To the silence
Note the rhythm
Feel the pace
Break the prism

Freedom of Speech
For violent jeers
Acts of suppression
For so many years

Luring you to drink
Poison, your fate
Don't take the bait!
Let's lighten up our loads
Let's give up the hate

It's the only way out of here ...

Afternoon Updates at the Chancellor's Complex Occupation

Professor Widener, Mar Velez, Bryant Pena, David Ritcherson, March 1, 2010

Professor Widener: Just a couple of updates: discussions are continuing. I wont speak for anyone in the room, but sense is that things have been quite positive. The impact of your bodies, and your brains, and your voices, is being directly felt by each of us in there, in every second, so I want to first say "Thank you, again" to everyone outside.

I want to have one or two chants of a chant that we used to have back when we were fighting the apartheid movement, and we were taking over a lot of stuff, and the chant goes like this: "Inside, outside, all on the same side." So if we could have that a couple of times...

"INSIDE!" "OUTSIDE!" "ALL ON THE SAME SIDE!"
"INSIDE!" "OUTSIDE!" "ALL ON THE SAME SIDE!"
"INSIDE!" "OUTSIDE!" "ALL ON THE SAME SIDE!"

So we took a little break because there was a discussion, we wanted to come out and make sure there was good communication. .... We're about halfway through, and you haven't seen us storm out of there cussing and calling people names, so that's a good sign ... . I think David and Fnann might have a few things to say too ...

Okay so..it's up to folks—of course everything here is up to everyone. We're going back inside, and hopefully we'll be through fairly soon—(aside: can folks stay? Is that ...) ... . I'm not going to make that decision, that's for David, Fnann, Mar, Sam, some other [student] leadership folks, and I'm going to stop talking. I just want to say thank you again, to everybody ...

Mar Velez: I guess just to update y'all, we were meeting with administration...let's just say that—we're not going to say the demands have been met *yet*, but they are in the process of being met. Does that make sense? I just want to say, if any of the administration inside can hear me, thank you for meeting with us, because that just shows the first steps of your commitment. And that's what we need right now is commitment, from *them*. Because obviously we're committed just by us being out here. And your energy was definitely felt inside. OUR university.

David: Thank you, Mar. We had a slightly more productive meeting than last Friday. We were impressed, er..well…it was a big improvement from the last document they released to us. So they are working hard, and so are we. It is a collective effort, and we've recognized a few, several key people who make a lot of the decisions here at the university, so we've met with those individuals, we are in contact with them. There's going to be another follow-up meeting this Thursday at 9 am to address certain things that went on at this meeting, so we can kind of solidify everything and put it on paper: what *exactly* is going to happen, who *exactly* is going to be involved, when *exactly* it's going to happen. So the details of everything will be addressed Thursday at 9 am, but yeah—we are making progress, we are moving in the right direction. And it's because of everybody out here, it's because of y'all, it's because of us, it's because of the admin as well. I want to thank everybody. And Thursday is March 4th—there's a lot going on. You want to address that?

Bryant Pena: So hopefully at noon, when we all meet at Library Walk on March 4th, we'll be able to hear the results of that. We'll be able to meet up, and see if it's going to be a celebration, or—an, umm…you know what I'm saying?…. (laughter). A lot of classes are going to have public classes, and teach out on that day, there will be speakers, music, and finish up with a rally downtown. So see you Thursday.

And thank you for keeping it peaceful in the face of, you know, anyone coming to try to mess up what we're doing. Thank you for the roses, thank you for the love and the support. We really felt it in there—we're having a meeting, and the fact that you're here supporting us, that really meant a lot. Because it's really like we're all one, we're all a family, so thank you.

Bryant: So hopefully these demands will be fully met, but regardless, we still face an issue with the state, and a 32% increase to our tuition—so bear in mind that will be the core of Thursday. ... Because the whole state will be with us in saying that we need to keep the universities *public*.

David: Also, tonight: we're having a General Body meeting at the Cross [Cultural Center] at 6:30, for people who want to get more specific updates on what's going on. There will also be a "Know Your Rights" presentation, also a presentation on allyship, how to be a strong ally in the movement. Definitely come out...it will be fun, it will be fulfilling... Any final remarks from the crowd?

Crowd: "THANK YOU, STUDENT LEADERS!" (applause and laughter)

And we'll end with a unity clap. For those of you that it's your first time here....the history of the unity clap is something the farmworkers movement—Filipino farmworkers and Mexican farmworkers—in order for them to come together as one and communicate, and also silence their boss, they started clapping all together, slowly, and then faster and faster and faster, and at the end of that they would shout "ISANG BAGSAK!" which in Tagalog means, "One struggle down, one more to go!"

[whole crowd clapping, builds to a crescendo] ISANG BAGSAK!
HOLLA BACK! I GOT YOUR BACK!
HOLLA BACK! I GOT YOUR BACK!
HOLLA BACK! I GOT YOUR BACK!

Photo courtesy of Cutler Edwards.

PART 4

FUTURES

Photo courtesy of Zachary Kim.

UCSD BLACK STUDENT UNION PROTEST

At a rally on Library Walk, BSU members chanted for more than 5 minutes, while Chancellor Marye Anne Fox, Vice Chancellor of Student Affairs Penny Rue, and Chief Diversity Officer Sandra Daley looked on, February 19, 2010

REAL PAIN! REAL ACTION! REAL PAIN! REAL ACTION!

The University is an Apparatus

University Liberation Coalition pamphlet, first published March 4th 2010

I. THE U.C. IS A CORPORATE AND RACIAL APPARATUS

We, a concerned group of graduate students and our allies, have reached our limits. We are nauseous!

The particular racial acts committed during the last month contributed to our symptoms. Nooses, KKK hoods, and other racial threats have made us sick to the core.

Beyond that, our nausea stems from the weak responses made by the administration. Its feigned surprise at the racial state of emergency disgusted us. Despite years of warnings about the problem of systemic racism and the toxicity of the campus environment for minorities, the administration remained silent and unmoved. It took the public spectacle of racism and a tremendous amount of grassroots resistance to get them to listen. Their doors remained shut to the most marginalized members of the community—an occupation had to take place for those doors to open. This administration, which has continually placed corporate ambitions above the rights of students who have been admitted to the university without being included in it, has left us wondering: Who does this university support?

We are frustrated. Our nerves are frayed. Every push toward change from the bottom seems to be met with stubborn hostility from the top. Despite the struggles of generations of students and faculty fighting for a better and more inclusive UC system, a severe educational crisis remains. A corporate and racist shadow hangs over the university. Past activists have won decisive battles, but the war for our university and education remains at a frustrating standstill. Recent victories show what we are up against: After the administration finally agreed to the Black Student Union's demands, the validity of their agreement has been called into question. Lawyers try to stall the BSU victory. They incite the Law to knock the wind out of us, and stop us dead in our tracks. They hope to use the Law to continue policies that stifle the admission and retention of marginalized students. Negating the BSU's demands as unconstitutional, they will attempt to use legal tools to bolster systematic discriminatory practices. In conjunction with this troubling legal backlash, the institutional structure of the university, which privileges the needs of corporations over the needs of its students, remains in place. As long as this is intact, the university will continue to exploit and marginalize students of color, students from working class backgrounds, and queer students.

We cannot and will not accept these conditions. Sickened to the core, we still resist in the ways we know best—through words that are more powerful than weapons and through a liberatory pedagogy that counters hate and exclusion with lessons in hope.

Let it be known:

The UC system is an apparatus that shapes students and their thoughts within machinery that is patriarchal, homophobic, racially exclusionary, and classist. Diversity statistics fail to show the nuances of this apparatus. They fail to show that the university is guided by the corporate few for the benefit of the corporate few.

At all levels, this apparatus produces docile students, faculty members, and administrators who ignore or fail to see the State-supported corporate systems that are shaping not only students' lives and educations, but the very future of the UC system. We have all become part of this system, each one of us implicated within the government's privatized machinery that has stolen the name University of California.

Most distressingly, the UC apparatus grinds down instructors and professors who are working to transform oppressive institutions. Faced with a vast, unyielding apparatus, we become docile and complacent. We accept the impossibility of meaningful change. We are made to think that our roles within the apparatus are natural—that we do not have the right to think beyond University parameters and the corporate ideologies that the university has come to reflect and reinforce. When we demand real change, we do so with hesitance and unease because we cannot imagine such change occurring in the UC of the present. Our knowledge and cynicism cripple our ability to hope, to envision a future of new possibilities. This shortsightedness, this refusal of the power of futurity, keeps us trapped in the unending cycles of the apparatus—quarter follows quarter, year follows year. The apparatus traps us in its temporal framework, limiting our capacity to dream of what the UC could potentially become.

Worst of all, the university functions on tactics of turnover: The logic being that four to six years from now, we—the dedicated agents of change—will have graduated. Everything will return to business as usual. The subversive call to action may begin anew, but as history as shown, each cycle will have no staying power. The apparatus and its agents of corporate interest are quite comfortable treating our thoughts as temporary byproducts to be expelled after graduation. They are happy to see our so-called illusions and delusions broken by the temporality of the machine. They are content that our struggles have no continuity or lasting effect. They find solace in our inability to sustain our movements within their machinery.

As graduate students, we have come to see that our own docility implicates us in the corporate project of the UC system and its Board of Regents. Despite our best efforts, we teach students the corporate way. When we attempt to challenge the rules of the university apparatus, the system co-opts our thoughts, classifies our ideas as insignificant and dangerous delusions not meant for the classroom. We are dismissed as "aberrations" and "malcontents."

By rewarding the pursuit of individual success in the job market, the apparatus instructs our students to have selective hearing and selective seeing: they are taught to see the façade of the apparatus without seeing what lies beneath. They are made to hear only corporate white noise.

The machinery of the UC system shapes our students, molding their thoughts to advance and reflect corporate intentions and State ambitions. The apparatus pushes them toward what matters in society: the formulaic essay, the A, the degree, and other material labels that mark them as a fancy, well-decorated item to be purchased in the job market. An overwhelming number of students have arrived at the purpose of the university. Yet, they are unable to see how they were steered there and shaped into cogs in the corporate machine.

For too long, our students have been taught to acquiesce to this, the physics of the apparatus.

What no longer matters—what is no longer funded—are the practical tools that we can share with our students: the tools that will impart them with a deeper knowledge, an understanding of how the world spins and how they can change the spin of the world. What no longer matters is a liberatory education. And in this respect, the university is non-existent.

II. "OUR UNIVERSITY"

On February 24, 2010, an alarm was struck and a new community woke up at UCSD. On the steps of the Price Center, we the authors, became part of a community that is willing to take back the university on our own terms. There is necessary self-reflexivity in our phrasing here—our grammar marks a return of selfhood that has been denied to the objectified.

Photo courtesy of Jorge Narvaez.

Awakened, we saw the apparatus in full form. We became conscious and cognizant of it. And we saw that we are the potential for its collapse.

The pressure to break apart the corporate apparatus has come from below, from those groups who the administration has continually included on unequal and racist terms. At UC San Diego, Black students comprise 1.3% of the undergraduate population. For too long they have been considered an expendable byproduct within the machinery. For the agents of the apparatus, that figure has been of little concern. Until now.

The pressure to reclaim our university has risen up from the bottom, from those students that have been trod upon, spit on, and spit out of the apparatus on a daily basis. Those who were considered waste have surfaced. They have begun the call for radical change.

Black students, Chicano students, Chicanas, and other students of color are the first willing to shout "Our University!" Those who are excluded on campus because of their sexual orientation or class have woken up in solidarity. White, heterosexual, upper-class allies have become conscious and joined the visible ranks. Even our faculty and staff mentors, who have seen the battles of the past, have recognized something new underfoot.

The lines have been drawn around violence and pain.

We have come to see the violence unleashed from multiple levels of power, including racial student actions and responses, racial media campaigns, and the weak racial administrative responses to the state of emergency.

We have born witness to the pain recent events have inflicted on human beings. We have seen the Black students' pain of losing legitimacy in the eyes of their peers, their professors, and the administration. Along with this, we have seen Black students experience the pain of recognition: the cognitive awareness that people are willing to use words and play out stereotyped roles that prolong and perpetuate a history of racism and violence. We saw the exclusionary pain of the law, the frustration that came from individuals deploying free speech to cover up blatant hate speech. We saw the pain of misdirected policy: our administration forced guilt upon Black students by shutting down all campus media because of the real concern with racist media. And most recently, we could not avert our eyes from the pain caused by a symbol that rippled into history from the past: a noose.

Pain has produced a necessary tension. It has caused many to flinch. It has caused others to act and react. We have opened our eyes. We see even more clearly what we already felt on a subliminal level: that racism is systemic to the University of California; that racial exclusion is connected to a larger apparatus that supports an entrenched corporate agenda over the human rights of its most expendable students.

Some may not see those connections, perhaps because they have refused to witness the Black students' real pain. They may have seen the noose, but they have failed to see the shadow that extends from the past into our present.

We have seen the shadow.

We see, hear, and in some cases feel real violence and real pain. This is no longer just shadow play. This is real pain that affects real people.

Real pain will continue to drive our community's real action. In response to weak nooses, we have formed powerful bonds of solidarity. In response to hate speech, we have learned to articulate empowered radical speech. In response to inadequate administrative responses, we have taken up real action. In response to governmental corporate agendas, we refuse to let the material needs of the marginalized be pushed aside. We refuse to cede our agency to a State government willing to bail out banks before it bails out low-income communities and the poorly funded students of color that emerge from these communities. We demand more from a State government that is more active in providing corporations with access to student consumers than it is in providing marginalized students with access to the university.

Pain will continue to drive us, a select but growing number of graduate students, toward a real pedagogy that goes beyond the classroom.

As concerned graduate students—more importantly as members of a new university community within the UC—we affirm our beliefs here: No longer will we be dictated by corporate ambitions and the exclusionary systems that have come to shape our educations and lives. Our thoughts will no longer be filtered. Rather, we will share our tools with students of color and their allies who are putting aside their academic work for the more pressing work of defending their human rights and legitimacy at the university. At the same time, we will gain new tools from them, which will steer our pedagogical approaches in the years to come. Our lives are aligned. Our theory and practice are one.

The apparatus will attempt to shape us, the instructors and students of the next generation, within its parameters of corporate time and space. But it cannot steal our thoughts, our words, and their real effect. We have come to know our own place. In covert ways we will work within the parameters of the apparatus to undermine those limitations. The agents of the machine will not recognize us because we will keep up the facade. We will exploit the law and hide behind it to achieve the opposite objective of the supremacists who hide behind free speech. We will use all available technologies to build social networks of resistance, to communicate in unrestricted ways, and to support each other across the fracture lines the apparatus has used to divide our university communities. Our masquerade is different than their racial minstrels. Underneath it all, we will remain a continuous presence—a constant disruption within the machine—that wages our nonviolent guerilla war to remake our university from the ground up.

III. ANTI-REGENCY

The apparatus seeks to alienate us from one another, to prevent us from forming bonds of solidarity. Departmental lines have kept us broken. But now a hidden substratum of community unites us. We ask our allies across departments to heed the call to reclaim the university on our terms of inclusivity and justice.

Our growing community is an anti-regency. No one reigns for us. No one reigns over our thoughts or gestures. We will not be spoken for. We will not be policed, corporatized, or privatized in our academic work, political work, and pedagogical work. However, since race still matters, we will maintain an inclusionary politics of interracial solidarity, which will be our strength and counter-balance to the weight of the apparatus. Beyond March 4 2010, we will bring our presence back to the absent university. We will find and fight for the return of a university that we have never known.

Agents of the status quo believe that such resistance will go away. They hope that the backbone of our community will be broken when it runs up against the university's exclusionary walls. They believe that by stalling and creating enough obstacles, the movement will bow beneath the sheer weight of an entrenched bureaucratic order. This is how the UC apparatus operates: Inertia is how it resists change.

Inactivity and docility, on the part of its students, administrators, and staff, is how the apparatus perpetuates age-old inequalities and divisions. But inactivity will not be tolerated when it prolongs exploitation and oppression. Nor will inactivity be the death of our movement. A desire to maintain business as usual will be met by our continual demand for change – a demand that will boil to the surface whenever and wherever it is necessary, whether it is in the classroom or chancellor's office.

Let it be known:

Our gestures are marked by a radical love. Our clenched fists hold flowers and chalk and pens. These will be the most effective counter tools to nooses and coercive corporate plans in this battle for the university. Our words and our writing are the weapons we will use— these are the gestures that the apparatus cannot efface or expel over time. Through mentorships and critical pedagogy, we will overcome the temporal limitations of turnover by creating new generations of activists who will sustain our resistance.

We take up radical love not as an abstract value, but as a concrete means of resistance. We express it not through words, but through actions that recognize the humanity of the students that the apparatus regards as expendable goods. Our love is not self-sacrificial. It does not make concessions to a corrupt and corrupting educational system. Instead, it recognizes the liberatory potential of a university system that prioritizes and invests in all of its students rather than corporate ambitions and greed.

Our community creates and sustains its own energy. That energy cannot be touched. It has already changed our pedagogy and our lives. Our fire of peaceful resistance has been kindled within an oppressive university apparatus. Some have mistaken it for a small anomalous flame that has touched only a few students and faculty. Do not be mistaken—this fire is spreading. It is burning away worn out educational values and tired pedagogies and forging something new. And now, that fire will burn at that apparatus from the bottom up. It will be hard for anyone or institution to put out a fire that burns on the inside. It will be even harder to quell a fire that is productive rather than destructive, inclusive rather than exclusive—the people will recognize the justice in our gestures of radical love and the injustice that marks the desire to stomp us out of a failing apparatus.

In Solidarity, Love and Hope,
University Liberation Coalition

Professor Jorge Mariscal, Literature, BSU Press Conference

February 24, 2010

Buenos Dias. Let me say something before I begin that was said in 1967 by a group of activists trying to change this country and end a war: "Black and Brown together forever, as long as the moon and sun shall shine."

Once upon a time, there was a city, surrounded by levies. And the people in the most vulnerable part of the city kept telling the officials in charge that they were in danger, that the levies weren't strong, that something might happen. And the people in power kept saying, "don't worry about it, we're all on the same boat, if something happens it will affect us all equally." And then one year a storm blew in. And by the time it hit the city the storm wasn't that strong, but it was strong enough to weaken the levies. And the levies broke. And not everyone was devastated, but the people who had been warning about the weak levies were devastated.

Photo courtesy of Cutler Edwards.

This university is that city. People have been warning the administrations over time that control this university that the levies were weak, that the climate was hostile, that the curriculum did not reflect those communities. I can tell you today with all sincerity that the administration of UCSD deserves what it's getting. It's not easy for me to say that—I've spent 24 years of my life at this institution—but it's true. And just as in New Orleans, when the levies broke, some people were held accountable for dereliction of duty. And I want to tell you today that somebody at the top of this university needs to be held accountable for dereliction of duty …

Literature Department Statement

February 28, 2010

The Literature Department supports the recent proposals by UCSD faculty of African descent and the UCSD Black Student Union. We are their allies in calling for UCSD to address racial inequities as it restructures the university during the budget crisis.

We urge a full systematic analysis of the recent racist acts at UCSD, which are reflective of a university system that has not yet created the conditions for racial equity. Fifteen years after Proposition 209, the repeated instances of racism by UCSD students, and also the administration's inability to address them effectively, testify to the need for the university to renew its commitments to public access and inclusion for students, faculty, and staff from historically underrepresented communities. As we work to preserve higher education as a public good, we must also secure resources to support curriculum, research, and scholarship on the critical study of race and racism, as well as greater outreach and changes to admissions, resource allocation, and college requirements so the university can create an academic culture that prepares a diverse public to participate in and contribute to a multiracial society.

In the days ahead, the Department encourages instructors to address the crisis with their students. Moreover, the Department will do its best to accommodate those students whose academic work has been disrupted by the recent racist incidents, and urges the University to make every effort to assure the safety and security of students, staff, and faculty at UCSD.

Letter to Sociology Graduate Students

Professor Ivan Evans, Sociology, February 25, 2010

[Socgrad] Please circulate

ivan evans ievans at ucsd.edu

Thu Feb 25 16:07:44 PST 2010

- Previous message: [Socgrad] March 4th Teach-Outs - Survey
- Next message: [Socgrad] Fwd: noose in campus library
- **Messages sorted by:** [date] [thread] [subject] [author]

Dear grads:

The 4th of March next week is a big day for the UC system—especially for all of us who believe in public education and are resolved to prevent the privatization of the UC system. We will do everything possible---and then some--to prevent the conversion of the UC into the exclusive plaything of a small elite, almost out of reach of the middle class and a mere pipe-dream for poorer households. Privatization would blithely destroy diversity of all sorts and reverse the painstaking gains that have been made in California over the past four decades.

The battle has just begun.

We are still fumbling for an effective alternative. Each campus is still isolated and so, collectively, we are not yet sure how to settle on a common state-wide strategy. But we do know that the "restructuring" juggernaut has to be stopped before it crystallizes. That would at least buy us time to figure out our strategy.

Meanwhile, universities are responding to the budget crisis (if that is what it is) by resorting to a "facts on the ground" approach that is slowly ensnaring universities in the logic of privatization and neo-liberalism. Staff are being released. Non-Senate faculty ("lecturers") without Security of Employment (SoE) are already being phased out--and re-hired as ad hoc, cheap labor.

Support for graduate students is decreasing. The number of undergraduate admissions is being scaled back … Departments, the institutions to which that graduate students and faculty are most bonded, have been compelled to cannibalize themselves. And so we witness the tawdry sight of faculty looking round for someone to fire in order to save themselves. The list of shame goes on and on.

Yet, even as the university is being radically "restructured", evidence mounts that at least part of the "budget crisis" is no more than a manufactured crisis, the artifice of shady book-keeping tricks and a less-than-transparent budgeting process. In the '90s, the UC acted on the

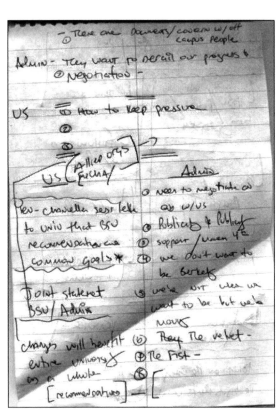

advice of snake-oil financial advisors and plunged into make-a-quick-buck deals. Until a few days ago, for example, almost no-one knew that the UC speculates in real estate investments in Tahiti … Tahiti?! Now that the bubble has burst, the pain is simply passed off to ordinary Californians--who had no clue that some of their tax dollars were buying up expensive real estate in places such as Tahiti. Meanwhile, the number of senior administrators exploded as managers turned the UC system into a trough for feeding cronies and, of course, ever more senior administrators. And so a movement is afoot to compel the UC to come clean on the budgeting process.

The "facts on the ground" approach that is picking off departments one by one has to be stopped. We need much more non-biased information about the state of the budget and precisely HOW it operates. But we cannot wait for solutions to wend their way into law. The juggernaut has to be crippled now.

Please do all that you can to educate students about events planned for the 4th of March! Print out the leaflets and hand them out to your students. Explain why threats to the UC threaten the value of each student's degree. Exhort them not to pull up the ladder as they exit UC--there are many more equally deserving candidates who deserve admission to what is, after all, still a public institution.

I am attaching flyers that each of you can copy and hand out starting Monday next week. Print as many as you can. Stand on the pathways. Take to Library Walk. Go into the Price Center and the Libraries--and leaflet, leaflet, leaflet!

Ivan

UCSD Music Department Response to Racist Incidents on Campus

The UCSD Music Department has taken note of the recent string of racially charged events on and around campus with revulsion and deep concern. We support the "Faculty Statement on Racism and Campus Climate at UCSD," the various statements of other departments, and the actions of the Black Student Union. Numerous discussions have taken place within Music amongst faculty and students, and we are in the process of examining our own policies. A short statement from the perspective of the Music Department follows.

As a public institution, our responsibility is to teach and practice critical engagement with the complex fabric of American culture. A pervasive obliviousness and insularity within our community seems to us the background to the horrendously insensitive and hurtful actions of the last weeks; but recent events have escalated from stupidity to outright bigotry.

A public university has a mission to address historical inequality. While efforts to diversify our campus have obviously been made, the statistics on student and faculty demographics remain embarrassing. We need to acknowledge our failures, and be accountable for addressing them, both collectively and individually. We must all take individual responsibility for educating ourselves about racism, sexism, classism, homophobia, and other forms of structural inequality.

Issues of culture, ethnicity, and institutional power lie at the foundation of the study of music, and we have a responsibility to engage them. The Music Department currently offers immersive courses in diverse practices of music-making; an undergraduate major in musics of the African diaspora; and numerous lecture courses examining American popular traditions and world musics. There is still more that we can do. Music can be a powerful catalyst for outreach, and we recognize the urgent need to reach younger students in the San Diego community, before assumptions about inequality or destructive stereotypes are irreversibly ingrained. We must intensify our support of these efforts, but we need institutional backing for the sustainability of these programs.

The current fiscal crisis raises the stakes. We are now reaping the results of years of not-so-benign neglect when it comes to enrolling and graduating students from historically underrepresented demographics. Any serious effort to remedy this neglect will require money and resources. The budget crisis makes this highly challenging, but cannot excuse us from responsibilities that cut to the core of our mission as a public institution. Moves to aggressively raise fees and target out-of-state enrollment will further reduce access for underrepresented students. The future of our university depends on decisions made in the immediate future, and we are committed to assuming responsibility for whatever role we can take in this process.

100th Love Poem for Students of Color

Vejea Jennings, an alumnus, a former BSU board member,
a professor, a motion in the Movement

black / brown / yellow mindstrokes genius
canvas me a campus fingerprint a fist in public
in the face of what's missing us and them / immense
black / brown / yellow brilliant well-read / earth-bred
research me a future pen tomorrows in obsidian
in sienna in amber then recite it aloud
into the mouths of children into the ears of elders
and our communities will be better for it

black / brown / yellow shades imagine
dream with your hands act with your minds
question the answers color a campus
rainbow a moment then tone it black
magic it brown burn it yellow
and our communities will be better for it

black / brown / yellow sound back
echo all that you learn gift us urgency and more
we adore you black / brown / yellow
and we know we support you
with hearts of hard silk
with minds of new fabric
and our communities will be better for it

Photo courtesy of Erik Jepsen.

Dialoguing Across Difference and Privilege

Elizabeth Sine, March 3, 2010

A letter from Elizabeth Sine, PhD Student, US History at UC San Diego (and by proxy from many of us, I think, an outgrowth of a long and ongoing conversation):

Dear Allies, those I know and those I don't (ie., whomever may read this):

Before and above all else, I want to thank the BSU, MEChA, and everyone else who helped to ignite the movement taking place on our campus, and who have helped to open up some real maneuvering room within this university for all of us who want to transform it and to make it a fully public institution. I write today not only in celebration of the struggle we are currently engaged in, today, these past few weeks, and—for many of us, in varying ways—for a long time before that, but also with an eye toward the long haul we have ahead.

Like many have already noted, the diversity of coalitions and people who have come together to support this movement, and to support the demands laid out by the BSU, is remarkable. The effort to challenge the racialized hierarchy that holds this institution together, and to combat the ongoing process of the university's privatization, has brought together so many people, across lines of racial and cultural difference, and across the ranks assigned to us by the university system—undergraduate students, graduate students, faculty, staff. I want to address the question of how we might continue to build and engage in meaningful dialogue and common struggle across lines of difference, with particular attention to varying forms of privilege and underprivilege attached to those differences. More specifically, I want to raise some issues and questions for students committed to the struggle for greater diversity in the university who are operating from positions of privilege—white privilege or otherwise.

I think most who read this will recognize the institutional nature of the racism, classism, sexism, and homophobia that the student movement aligns itself against. I think many recognize the uneven and hierarchical nature of the distribution of power in our university system, as well as the extent to which the ongoing corporatization of UCSD in particular, and public education in general, threatens to intensify already-existing inequalities and modes of oppression (with a particularly menacing threat to underrepresented groups within our community). And I think that it's important to acknowledge, and to become comfortable thinking and talking about, the implications of the university's hierarchical structure for internal relations within our movement—what it means to engage in struggle, in a coalition as diverse as ours, against an institution that has been designed to privilege some at the expense of others.

Indeed, it is vital for all of us to understand that the problems of racism and inequality are collective, and that every person here has an important role to play in the struggle against the denial of human dignity and for institutional change. At the same time, the institutions of privilege and inequality that exist on this campus and in our society mean that we all approach this struggle from different vantage points and from a playing field that has never been even.

And so, for trust to exist among us and for the full strength or our collective action to be realized, I think we have to take fully into account the varying forms of privilege that come attached to our to our socioeconomic status, our racial and ethnic identifications, our gender and sexual practices, and whatever other factors affect our social position and relationship to each other. In fact, I would go even further to say that those among us whom this university has been designed to benefit bear a responsibility to think critically about, and to disinvest from, our own social advantages (beginning with a recognition that those advantages are not a pure result of our own hard work).

Surely, there are many among us who have been thinking about and working through these issues for a long time. But I think it's worth putting on the table for serious reflection and discussion in this critical moment in which new forms of solidarity are taking shape and when there is so much at stake. We have to be comfortable acknowledging the ways in which some one who is racialized as white (such as myself) cannot ever really understand the experience of racial oppression, even as we participate in the struggle against it. And so, for such individuals, the struggle against institutional racism must begin with a disinvestment from whiteness, from the advantages of middle-class upbringing—from whatever other advantages have been tied to the social positions we were born into.

So, what does this mean in practice? What does it take to disinvest from privilege—from white privilege, or class privilege, male privilege, or the privileges attached to normative sexual practices and identities? Of course, there is no simple or singular answer to these questions. But there may be a couple of starting points to build on.

To begin with, as I've already been suggesting, I think it will be difficult to move forward without making transparent the ways in which various forms of privilege operate across lines of difference within our coalition. Whether this occurs on the level of personal reflection, in the realm of political thinking, in our informal discussions with each other, I think it's important that the issue is brought out into the open.

Secondly, we must bring into a practice a politics of listening. It is way too easy, especially given the individualism promoted by our social institutions, to become absorbed in the way this struggle looks from a particular and personalized vantage point. The danger of this kind of individualist tendency is that it threatens our solidarity by blinding us to the ways in which multiple struggles are intersecting and overlapping in this movement, even as they all ultimately challenge inequality and corporatization in the university. Listening and taking seriously each other's needs and concerns will not only help to strengthen our solidarity and our movement but will help us to avoid reproducing the kinds of hierarchies that we are struggling to transform.

The disparities of power that shape relations across race, class, gender, and sexuality do not have to persist. But I believe that they can't be dismantled without our open acknowledgment of them, our critical and careful reflection on them, and a deliberate effort to extricate ourselves from them and to bring into practice a different kind of social relations that prioritizes the dignity of every one here, in ways that UCSD's administrative power structure has not.

Laying bare and discussing openly the hierarchies of privilege that shape our university—and the social, political, and economic institutions that dominate it—will be uncomfortable for some, but I can guarantee it's a lot less uncomfortable than enduring first-hand the kind of isolation, marginalization, and oppression that many students on our campus have been experiencing for a long time. And it is necessary to move forward together toward taking back our university.

In Solidarity,
Elizabeth Sine
Graduate Student
U.S. History

And I undersign myself.
Thank you for this work, Elizabeth.
Cutler Edwards
PhD Student, US History
UC San Diego

Unthinking the Nation

Maile Arvin, March 3, 2010

This past fall commemorated the 40ᵗʰ anniversary of the founding of Ethnic Studies led by the students of the Third World Liberation Strike at San Francisco State University. During that same fall of 1969, Alcatraz (officially designated "federal surplus land") was first occupied by a group of Native Americans, mostly college students. Their demands included greater political and land rights for Native Americans, an end to the damaging policy of tribal termination, and better access to quality health care, housing, and education—in short, nothing less than self-determination and the resources required to fulfill it for all Native Americans. The occupation lasted for nineteen months, until June 1971, and in conjunction with the American Indian Movement was partially successful in many of its goals.

Remembering Alcatraz is not invoked here as a nostalgic wish for the resistance movements of the past. For the last few weeks have proved that struggles for decolonization are ongoing and beautifully alive on our very own campus. When I first wrote part of this introduction as part of the materials for this colloquium series back in January, I ended this intro with some questions. This Winter colloquium series aimed to critically question the relationships Ethnic Studies has forged with and against the nation-state, especially in terms of the widening public/private divide that has many people of color at UC and other public university campuses again occupying buildings. Thus I asked: How do we achieve today not just reforms but radical overhauls in the various areas of public education, our particular disciplinary boundaries, and social justice for people of color more generally? In these times when governments insist funding cuts are essential, how do we reverse the discourse and reclaim, like those at Alcatraz, our "federal surplus"?

Though they were somewhat rhetorical questions when I first wrote them, I believe our campus' undergraduate student leaders have amply shown that our university can be reclaimed. Thus, though we had originally scheduled this colloquium to be a panel of graduate student papers that engaged decolonization in different arenas from uranium mining in the Southwest to presentations of Native people in museums, we felt our last colloquium event of the quarter would be better served by inviting the students who have so remarkably led us all in the exciting and exhausting intellectual and activist work of decolonizing this university. A day before March 4th's International Day of Action for Educational Justice, today we pause to celebrate and recognize incredible work of the last few weeks.

A Letter from the Cross Cultural Center

Edwina Welch, February 23, 2010

Dear CCC Community,

The last two weeks of racist, sexist, and classist events have deeply impacted the lives of students, staff, alumni, faculty, and community members who work with and support the Cross-Cultural Center. I applaud all the hard work of these individuals and the community who have shown great restraint and civility in the face of blatant hostile remarks and the not so subtle dismissals and denials that incidents like these are even harmful to individuals and UC San Diego as a whole. The straw man argument that pits free speech against community safety belies more insidious, structural questions about a campus climate where these kinds of actions arise in the first place.

Campus climate, particularly for students of color, has long been an area that has cried out for attention. The activities of the past two weeks call for a much deeper response, a response that goes to the heart of the UC San Diego educational environment. In the coming weeks students, staff, faculty, and administration have a particular opportunity to get to the root of campus climate issues. We have the opportunity to "lift the lid" on how the campus operates, how individual students live day to day in an isolating environment, how some students, staff, and faculty dismiss this experience, and how we as a community can change and build a better climate for all. It will be a tall order—systemic change is challenging and requires courage to explicitly name the issues and try different strategies toward deep change.

With their brave work and call to action, the Black students and many, many supporters are calling on the University and all of us to be courageous and live up to the Principles of Community the campus espouses. I stand in community with the students and these efforts and pledge to be a part of the solution. If you want to be a part of systemically changing the campus environment make sure your voice is heard.

In Community,

Edwina Welch,
Campus Diversity Office and Director,
UC San Diego Cross-Cultural Center

Photo courtesy of Curtis Marez.

Australian Exchange Student Nick Ryan Speaks to Fellow Students on Library Walk

The morning after the noose was found, February 26, 2010

My Name's Nick, I'm a white man, I also happen to be an Australian exchange student. And I didn't want anyone to leave here without understanding that your brothers and sisters, even down under, support you 110%. ... As Martin Luther King once said, 'There comes a time when silence becomes a very betrayal of our humanity.' And we can't be silent! And this involves small conversations with the person beside us, this involves large conversations with the people in front of us, this involves physical action. LOVE IS AN ACTION MY FRIENDS! It's not simply a feeling. It might start that way, but it needs to be an action, and an action which speaks to all around us. An action of love, of humility, and sometimes of getting up and telling people, "You know what? Frankly I'm pissed off, and I'm afraid!"... This is bullshit that people say "I have the *freedom* to say something as aggressive as hanging a noose."... WE have the freedom to feel *SAFE*! And we also have the god damn RIGHT to be equal!"

My message is short: The global community is standing with you! This will be—I promise you—the most cherished moment of my experience here, as a foreigner to America. To see the love, and the respect that is shared amongst all these people. And I hope, and I pray, that this isn't the last of these—that this continues.

PROFESSOR YEN ESPIRITU, CHAIR OF ETHNIC STUDIES, CALLS FOR A CAMPUS SHUTDOWN

After the noose is found, February 26, 2010

TO THE UNIVERSITY:
Dear all,

Please call on Chancellor Fox to declare a state of emergency and shut down the campus. Last night, a group of Black students had to spend the night at the Cross because they feared for their lives if they were going to try to make it home. This is NOT a university. Students should not fear for their lives while going to school.

It is fundamentally wrong that students and faculty of color have had to labor around the clock this past week, putting aside their study, their research, their teaching, their writing, while the rest of the campus continue as usual. It is fundamentally unfair. Who will give them back the lost hours? Who will compensate them for their always-uncompensated and unrecognized labor, in this case to birth an institution that is truly a place of LEARNING, in the most profound sense of that word.

We call on all of you–students, staff, faculty, union reps, librarians, and ESPECIALLY ADMINISTRATORS–to share in this labor.

Prof. Yen Espiritu,
Chair, Dept. of Ethnic Studies

TO THE CHANCELLOR:
Dear Chancellor Fox:

As a Full Professor who has spent her whole 20-year career at UCSD, as Chair of the Ethnic Studies Department, and as a woman faculty of color who has faced many indignities over the years, I write to ask you to exercise your leadership today to declare a state of emergency and close down the campus–in recognition of the shattered state that the campus is in.

Since the "Compton Cookout" incident, many students and faculty of color and their allies have devoted countless hours to do your/our job of teaching about racism on campus and of ensuring that UCSD lives up to its mission as a place of learning–in the most profound sense of that word.

Their labor–physical, mental, emotional, intellectual–goes uncompensated, unrecognized, and even mocked by the largely apathetic UCSD community. Because they have had to put aside their study, their teaching, their research, their writing, to do the university work, they will again bear the brunt of the costs of being at a university that views "diversity", at best, as a benign celebration of multiculturalism and "economic empowerment."

As many of us face down today in the shadow of a noose, we ask that you share in this labor and that you ask the ENTIRE community at UCSD to share in this labor. To not do so will be to benefit, once again, from the labor of the marginalized and maligned at UCSD.

Every crisis can bring forth great change. You have an opportunity to participate in this movement of change in a real and fundamental way. Please do so, or we risk a campus that will be deeply divided for years to come. The campus will be shut down, one way or another. It'd be in our best interest that you are the one to shut it down.

Sincerely,
Yen Le Espiritu,
Chair, Dept. of Ethnic Studies

CHEYENNE STEVENS LEADS STUDENT CHANTS ON LIBRARY WALK

Hundreds of students gather in response to a noose hung in Geisel Library Friday morning, February 26, 2010

SHUT! IT! DOWN! SHUT! IT! DOWN! SHUT! IT! DOWN! SHUT! IT! DOWN!
SHUT! IT! DOWN! SHUT! IT! DOWN! SHUT! IT! DOWN! SHUT! IT! DOWN!
SHUT! IT! DOWN! SHUT! IT! DOWN! SHUT! IT! DOWN! SHUT! IT! DOWN!
SHUT! IT! DOWN! SHUT! IT! DOWN! SHUT! IT! DOWN! SHUT! IT! DOWN!
SHUT! IT! DOWN! SHUT! IT! DOWN! SHUT! IT! DOWN! SHUT! IT! DOWN!
SHUT! IT! DOWN! SHUT! IT! DOWN! SHUT! IT! DOWN! SHUT! IT! DOWN!
SHUT! IT! DOWN! SHUT! IT! DOWN! SHUT! IT! DOWN! SHUT! IT! DOWN!
SHUT! IT! DOWN! SHUT! IT! DOWN! SHUT! IT! DOWN! SHUT! IT! DOWN!
SHUT! IT! DOWN! SHUT! IT! DOWN! SHUT! IT! DOWN! SHUT! IT! DOWN!
SHUT! IT! DOWN! SHUT! IT! DOWN! SHUT! IT! DOWN! SHUT! IT! DOWN!
SHUT! IT! DOWN! SHUT! IT! DOWN! SHUT! IT! DOWN! SHUT! IT! DOWN!
SHUT! IT! DOWN! SHUT! IT! DOWN! SHUT! IT! DOWN! SHUT! IT! DOWN!
SHUT! IT! DOWN! SHUT! IT! DOWN! SHUT! IT! DOWN! SHUT! IT! DOWN!
SHUT! IT! DOWN! SHUT! IT! DOWN! SHUT! IT! DOWN! SHUT! IT! DOWN!
SHUT! IT! DOWN! SHUT! IT! DOWN! SHUT! IT! DOWN! SHUT! IT! DOWN!
IF YOU DON'T SHUT IT DOWN, *WE'LL* SHUT IT DOWN! IF YOU DON'T
SHUT IT DOWN, *WE'LL* SHUT IT DOWN! IF YOU DON'T SHUT IT DOWN,
WE'LL SHUT IT DOWN! IF YOU DON'T SHUT IT DOWN, *WE'LL* SHUT IT
DOWN! IF YOU DON'T SHUT IT DOWN, *WE'LL* SHUT IT DOWN! IF YOU
DON'T SHUT IT DOWN, *WE'LL* SHUT IT DOWN! IF YOU DON'T SHUT IT
DOWN, *WE'LL* SHUT IT DOWN! IF YOU DON'T SHUT IT DOWN, *WE'LL*
SHUT IT DOWN! IF YOU DON'T SHUT IT DOWN, *WE'LL* SHUT IT DOWN!
IF YOU DON'T SHUT IT DOWN, *WE'LL* SHUT IT DOWN! IF YOU DON'T
SHUT IT DOWN, *WE'LL* SHUT IT DOWN! IF YOU DON'T SHUT IT DOWN,
WE'LL SHUT IT DOWN! IF YOU DON'T SHUT IT DOWN, *WE'LL* SHUT IT
DOWN! IF YOU DON'T SHUT IT DOWN, *WE'LL* SHUT IT DOWN! IF YOU
DON'T SHUT IT DOWN, *WE'LL* SHUT IT DOWN!

Photo courtesy of James Evans.

PENNY RUE, WHERE ARE YOU? ...

THE DYNAMICS OF PUBLIC SPACE

James Stout

James Stout: the dynamics of public space

James's Notes | Notes about James | James's Profile

---

the dynamics of public space
Wednesday, March 3, 2010 at 8:03pm

I saw some graffiti today, and it got me thinking. Someone had tagged racism under a stop sign, so it read "stop racism", crafty. We live in a country, and a university where public space is institutionally controlled, it's our environment but on their terms. As many of you know i'm studying the use of street art to oppose dictatorship in Spain, there's no reason why we can't use public spaces to fight the norms here.

In recent days and weeks public space in this university has been dominated by hatred, whether hanging nooses in the library, putting hoods on statues or holding parties with hateful themes the space which we all occupy is being monopolised by a minority. Even "neutral" spaces aren't accurate reflections of our community. we have one mural and it's painted on a temporary canvas so we can take it down if it proves too political. Meanwhile we're surrounded by orders "stop" "no cycles or skateboards" "no parking" "drive inside the lines", "no fun", "think inside the lines".

So tomorrow, on a day we take action for public education, why not take action for public space as well. Make where you live beautiful and make it yours. use colours, posters, flowers, whatever you want. We're at a great turning point for our university right now and this is the best chance we'll get to really make it ours, so take it. We're students, we're good at manipulating words and images, so lets do what they did in Paris while our university was still in its infancy and make the space our own. Like i have said a million times before, if you define yourself against something, you only last as long as it does, if you stand for something, you cam make it last forever so stand up and claim your own space and identity not just against someone else claiming it.

peace

Written about 2 weeks ago · Comment · Like · Report Note

Professor Daniel Widener, History, Speaks at Student Movement Gathering

Cross Cultural Center, March 10, 2010

I think it's not that often that you get an experience that will go on past us, and that other people will remember, but I want everyone to know that they've experienced history in the past three or four weeks. We've made history. And hopefully, we'll continue going on, making more and more history, and writing new chapters. I've seen a lot of bravery; I've seen a lot of creativity; and I've seen a lot of pain and alienation. I've seen a lot of people engage in things that they didn't really come here to do, and become something other that who they thought they were or what they thought they were gonna do. One of the things about teaching here is, you know, when I went to college I didn't know what I was gonna do, or what I was gonna be, er … I won't say when I grow up because I haven't done that yet—I'm trying to avoid that as much as possible—but I always note, when I meet undergraduate students here, often times they already know what they're gonna do when they leave UCSD. You know, people already have this idea. And I feel like one of the things that I've seen, and felt, and experienced the last couple of weeks is people *opening themselves*, even as we've started to open up the university, to the possibility that all of us might become *something different than who we were, or who we imagined ourselves to be*. And that's been a really amazing thing that I've really felt honored and proud to witness.

And I also just want to note, as one of the people who's gotten a lot of attention, I want to echo what Professor Kaplan has said about the way that all of us are together—and that the parts that each of us plays in this are not permanent parts. Some people reduce their activity, some people graduate, some people hang around forever. And that the most important things for social movements, the most important thing for what we have is, again, *communication, trust*—that we find ways to open up the spaces where we're not comfortable, where we see problems, where we left something feeling like it wasn't too good—and that we use that to go even into a new direction.

And let me just say one more thing and then I'll shut up. When we seized the chancellor's complex—I shouldn't say we, because I was sitting inside of meetings all day—when all of *you* did that, you know, we were in negotiations. That was the day they gave us a very unsatisfactory piece of paper back ... . It wasn't gonna work as a final paper. They turned something else back to us that the students graded about a B+. So, you know, that'd get a degree, but it isn't excellent. Anyway, when you seized the chancellor's complex, a couple things happened that really unblocked what was going on inside the room. Um, and yet there were people in that room, and they didn't feel like there was a lot of communication between those of us who were talking inside with the bigwigs, the people who were mobilized in the courtyard, the people who had seized the chancellor's complex. And that was really my responsibility. And at a certain point, because it was 5 o'clock and because we could tell that the administration had sort of exhausted its capacity to think for the week, and we needed to give them a little more time, I said, "well maybe, you know, everyone should leave the building." And so people looked around, and I said, "well, go get people out." And that was really an opportunity for us to salute the people who had shown through their courage that they were prepared to go to jail. And we sort of had people come out, and it wasn't really in a celebratory way. It wasn't the way that it should have been. And some people came up to me afterward and they said, "you know, that could have been different. It could've been done better." It could've been done in a different way that would have really made people who had gotten themselves to a certain place of courage and strength aware that everybody outside knew what they were doing, and that the people outside were also prepared to defend them.

So I wanted to tell that story, to say that in the last three or four weeks there's been some mistakes that people have made. On our side, we've made some mistakes because we were too busy. We've made other mistakes because some of us are doing this for the first time. We've made other mistake because some of us just have limitations to our capacity. And so I want us to understand that all of the progress, and all of the victory, and all of the success we've made up to this point … it's happened even though we haven't been perfect. There's things we can improve on. And if what happens, that I suspect is gonna happen, which is that we have to continue to press the university to hold up and to extend what it's indicated that it might be willing to do—if we have to re-mobilize, and we have to figure out new tactics and new ideas—then we will be better. Because one of the things that's important for us to be able to do is to have spaces of dialogue, to acknowledge our mistakes, and to own up to them, and to thank people for pointing them out, and to figure out together how we can come back, in the coming weeks and the coming months, even stronger. Can we build something that will last here years? Can we make this place that has been so bad to all of us a point of resistance for the entire United States? Can we rebuild something here that will extend throughout the state, throughout the country, throughout the world? And I think that we can. I think that we can.

And I feel like we're on the cusp of something, and if we can hold together, trust each other, love each other, believe in each other, fight for each other, then it can be something that, five years from now, ten years from now, fifteen years from now, you're gonna tell people you were at UCSD, and they're gonna say, *we have a struggle here, what should we do?* And that's the important piece of what Professor Kaplan said. Each of you is a leader. Each of you is a revolutionary. Each of you is an agent of change. We should be able to go to Meridian, Mississippi, go to Oakland, to be able to go to South Bronx, to be able to go to Des Moines, to Milwaukee, and every person here should be able to say, this is how you crack the other side, this is what you need, this is what you're looking for. So what I'd like us to do in the spring: with one hand we fight the university, with the other hand we try to figure out what we need to learn, so that we can make this the core of movement that will change the United States. That's my vision, that's my dream. That's the change I want to be a part of.

UC Center for New Racial Studies Statement— Racism in the UC System

March 1, 2010

Antiracism demonstration at UCSD

Recent events at campuses throughout the University of California system confirm the rationale of the Center for New Racial Studies, a multicampus research program scheduled to be launched this coming academic year. Neither our society nor the UC system are "beyond race." Racial exclusion, racial stratification, and racial profiling have been refortified by the university's "postracial" claims. Education and research on the history of race and the critical study of racism are therefore more necessary than ever. We understand that "racism" is historically produced by social and institutional relations of power, and that "antiracism" includes practices that work to end discrimination, bigotry, and exclusion. So the call from the UCSD Faculty of African descent and Black Students Union for the university to address institutionalized racial inequity, the appeal by Muslim and Arab students being prosecuted for civil disobedience at UCI, and the efforts of students throughout the UC system to defend public access to education—all deserve our support as antiracist practices.

There are those who claim that recent incidents of campus racism are unrepresentative of the UC, or that they are the isolated actions of a misguided few. We suggest, to the contrary, that the incidents at UCSD, UCI, and elsewhere should be understood within local, national, and global racial context. UC's increasing privatization, its exclusion of poor and underrepresented groups, and its dismissal of racist attacks as isolated events, should be viewed as evidence that the university's approach to race and racism has become incoherent and contradictory. UC is supposedly not taking race into account in admissions decisions, which results in sharp declines in Black and Latin@ access to higher education in California. Meanwhile insults and threats are directed at the few Black students who remain. Are we to believe these patterns—exclusion and attacks—are not intimately related?

The confused and ineffective response to racist incidents such as those at UCSD signals a retreat from the university's commitment to produce knowledge for the public good. It is not only racism at our campuses but UC's denial of access to students of color which generates these "incidents." Abandonment of UC's obligations to the people of California—a state whose population is now "majority-minority"—testifies to the need for a "new racial studies," as well as new public service in respect to race and racism. Addressing this need is essential if we are to create and sustain the conditions in which our universities can prepare diverse students to participate in a multiracial and increasingly global society.

BSU Update

March 6, 2010

To all our supporters:

First, let us express a sincere thank you to all of those who have had our back over the last two weeks. Together, we are working to transform UCSD into the kind of public university it was intended to be—accessible and welcoming to students from all communities; a resource for our people and all the people of California.

Some have said that we have exploited the crisis on campus in order to "get things for ourselves." Please know that the demands we made were intended to benefit all students, of every color and background. We more than most were deeply affected by the string of racist incidents. The structural changes we propose will help to create a university where such incidents can never again have the powerful impact we have witnessed for two long weeks.

This is not a Black thing; it is not even a Black-Brown thing. The 19 demands are designed to create a campus climate, support services, and curriculum that will enhance the educational experience of all students. How can it be that at one of the most prestigious universities in the world, a student can announce that she did not know that a hangman's noose was "an issue"? How can graduates of UCSD claim to understand the world if they are ignorant of their own country's history and if they have never had an African American or Native American classmate?

On Thursday, March 4, BSU signed an agreement with Chancellor Marye Anne Fox. In that agreement, the administration offered to take up each of our 19 demands and convert them into "common goals."

We are cautiously optimistic.

We are optimistic because we know that this is an historic moment. For decades, UCSD has been told that for many students the campus is not the utopia it pretends to be. Now is the time for the change to begin.

We are cautious because we understand that promises on a piece of paper, even one signed by the Chancellor, may not become reality or may become a misshapen distortion of what was intended. Promises can disappear never to be seen again into a bureaucracy that knows only its old ways.

This week a delegation from the Office of the UC President will arrive on campus to discuss implementation of the agreement. Forces from off campus are moving to disrupt the progress that has been made but we will not be distracted.

And so we ask that you remain vigilant and we ask for your continued support. What will UCSD look like in 20 or 30 years? None of us knows. But what we do know is that our generation has the responsibility to push the process of democratic educational change forward.

Real pain! Real action!
How long? Not long?
Real pain! Real action!

—

Black Student Union at UC San Diego

UC San Diego–Black Student Union Agreement

March 4, 2010

UC San Diego agrees to carry out the initiatives stated in the document dated March 4, 2010, entitled UC San Diego Administrative Commitments to Improve Campus Climate, as discussed throughout this week in the meetings of March 1 and March 4. We agree that additional changes will be made by mutual agreement to reflect the discussion that occurred today. This reflects the common goals presented by the Black Student Union regarding campus climate.

_____
Marye Anne Fox, Chancellor, UC San Diego

March 4, 2010

_____
David Ritcherson, Chair, Black Student Union

March 4, 2010

Photo courtesy of Erik Jepsen.

Acknowledgments

Without the support and activism of UC San Diego students, faculty, staff, and community members beyond the campus, who donated their speeches, poems, photographs, and personal writings, this book project would not have been possible. We want to thank those who contributed materials and thoughts to this ongoing project, including those whose words we were unable to include, and the many whose work took forms that cannot be represented on paper.

Holla back!

This is the inaugural publication of the **Center for Global California Studies**. It illustrates the Center's commitment to collaborative activist research, exemplified by the Another University is Possible Editorial Collective.

In addition to the Center for Global California Studies, we gratefully acknowledge the generous support of the UC San Diego History Department, Ethnic Studies Department, Chicano/a and Latino/a Arts and Humanities minor, and the African American Studies minor.

RESOURCES

FOR FURTHER INFORMATION AND RESOURCES ON THE STRUGGLE, PLEASE SEE:

- http://realpainrealaction.org
- http://stopracismucsd.wordpress.com
- http://ucsdcoalitionforeducationaljustice.wordpress.com
- http://savingucsd.ning.com

PHOTOS AND VIDEOS OF THE MOVEMENT IN PROGRESS MAY BE FOUND AT:

- http://www.flickr.com/groups/justiceucsd/
- http://www.youtube.com/justiceucsd

To contribute to the collection—such as poems, journal entries, fliers, buttons, photos, video, or any other materials—being archived in honor of responses to the campus climate, please contact UC San Diego's Archive of Knowledge at:

- archiveofknowledge@gmail.com